Yes, yes, yes! It is high time we rethink our emphasis on human leadership that has led to so much ministry failure and realign the church as a body under the headship of Christ. I pray we have the courage and humility to make the hard shifts that such realignment requires. Thanks to Lance Ford for issuing a challenge to us all.

**ANGIE WARD, PhD,** director, Doctor of Ministry and associate professor, Leadership and Ministry, Denver Seminary; author, *Uncharted Leadership: 20 Case Studies to Help Ministry Leaders Adapt to Uncertainty*

Prophets ask questions that get to the heart of the matter. In that tradition, Lance Ford skillfully, and with great care, questions the underlying assumptions of our current leadership paradigm, rightly diagnosing that the problem is in the very systems we have uncritically adopted in the church. Like a seasoned prophet, he doesn't just diagnose and deconstruct; he lays out a preferable future for us to consider, one where Jesus shoulders the burden—a must-read for our day.

**JR WOODWARD,** movement leader, V3; author, *The Scandal of Leadership: Unmasking the Powers of Domination in the Church*

*The Atlas Factor* is a biblically informed, prophetic rebuke to a far too worldly-informed leadership construct within the church. You may not agree with all that Lance has written, but you will do well to humbly read and reconsider your own view on leadership. I personally can attest to how the "atlas factor" has brought great harm to me and sadly to others through me. In light of all that we see happening with abusive and toxic leadership today, this book is for such a time as this.

**JEFF VANDERSTELT,** executive director, Saturate; author, *Gospel Fluency, Saturate,* and *One Eighty: A Return to Disciple-Making*

Lance Ford has been at the forefront of a call to reexamine our models of leadership and reorient the church to Jesus as its Head, not the "solo-heroic leader" so loved by a previous generation. As he's done this, one such leader after another has fallen from their pedestal, only confirming Ford's insistence that we rehabilitate and realign the church's leadership to its original design. An extremely sobering but inspiring book. The final chapter, which is full of practical steps, is worth the price alone.

**MICHAEL FROST,** Morling College, Sydney

In this unnervingly prophetic book, Lance exposes how modern concepts of solo-heroic, celebrity-loaded leadership effectively displace Jesus as the only Head of the church, resulting in dysfunctional leadership that attempts to carry a load we were never meant to carry. This book invites us to a necessary correction to the way that we conceive of, as well as implement, leadership in the church.

**ALAN HIRSCH,** author of numerous books on missional leadership, organization, and spirituality; cofounder, Movement Leaders Collective and the 5Q Collective

Lance has nailed it! The current forms and imports of leadership are not only ineffective in empowering the church to see more apprentices of Jesus, but they are also fostering an epidemic of burnout of leaders within the church. They are forms that Jesus never intended and have led us to an inauthentic expression of the church. *The Atlas Factor* is not only a worthy read, but it also helps us to continue to break free from our intoxication with leadership models birthed in our culture and realigns us back to the leadership of Christ.

**TERRY WALLING,** founder, Leader Breakthru; author, *Unlikely Nomads*

In *The Atlas Factor*, Lance Ford has put into words what I have been sensing about the Western church. Having witnessed the powerful move of God in the underground house churches in Iran, I have been concerned about the leadership business model of the American church, the loss of influence in our culture, and the epidemic of abuse. Thankfully in this book, Lance provides practical ways the church can move toward health and better impact the world for the gospel.

**NAGHMEH ABEDINI PANAHI,** author, *I Didn't Survive: Emerging Whole After Deception, Persecution, and Hidden Abuse*

Lance not only provides an understanding of the weaknesses in our prevailing leadership models but also reveals the biblical path to healthy, life-giving frameworks. For the tired and weary leader, this book is a must for your collection!

**L. ROWLAND SMITH,** national director, Forge America Mission Training Network; adjunct faculty, Denver Seminary and Fuller Seminary; author, *Life Out Loud: Joining Jesus Outside the Walls of the Church*

This is *the* book for this very moment. I now want to learn how to fly, just so I can airdrop thousands of copies and scatter *The Atlas Factor* all over American churches. It's that good and that important. Yes, yes, yes, to all of this! Thank you, Lance Ford.

**BRANT HANSEN,** radio host; author, *Unoffendable, Blessed Are the Misfits, The Truth About Us, The Men We Need,* and *Life is Hard, God is Good, Let's Dance*

# THE
# ATLAS
# FACTOR

LANCE FORD

# THE ATLAS FACTOR

SHIFTING
LEADERSHIP
ONTO

THE
SHOULDERS
OF JESUS

100 MOVEMENTS
PUBLISHING

First published in 2024 by 100 Movements Publishing
www.100mpublishing.com
Copyright © 2024 by Lance Ford

The author has no responsibility for the persistence or accuracy of URLs for external or third-party internet websites referred to in this book, and does not guarantee that any content on such websites is, or will remain, accurate or appropriate.

Some names have been changed to protect the privacy of individuals and organizations.

Library of Congress Control Number: 2023921052

All Scripture quotations, unless otherwise indicated, are from the ESV® Bible (The Holy Bible, English Standard Version®), © 2001 by Crossway, a publishing ministry of Good News Publishers. Used by permission. All rights reserved.

Scripture quotations marked MSG are taken from *The Message*, copyright © 1993, 2002, 2018 by Eugene H. Peterson. Used by permission of NavPress. All rights reserved. Represented by Tyndale House Publishers.

Scripture quotations marked NASB are taken from the (NASB®) New American Standard Bible®, Copyright © 1960, 1971, 1977, 1995, 2020 by The Lockman Foundation. Used by permission. All rights reserved. lockman.org

Scripture quotations marked NIV are taken from the Holy Bible, New International Version®, NIV®. Copyright © 1973, 1978, 1984, 2011 by Biblica, Inc.™ Used by permission of Zondervan. All rights reserved worldwide. www.zondervan.com. The "NIV" and "New International Version" are trademarks registered in the United States Patent and Trademark Office by Biblica, Inc.™

Scripture quotations marked NKJV are taken from the New King James Version®. Copyright © 1982 by Thomas Nelson. Used by permission. All rights reserved.

Scripture quotations marked NLT are taken from the *Holy Bible*, New Living Translation, copyright © 1996, 2004, 2015 by Tyndale House Foundation. Used by permission of Tyndale House Publishers, Carol Stream, Illinois 60188. All rights reserved.

Scripture quotations marked RSV are from the Revised Standard Version of the Bible, copyright © 1946, 1952, and 1971 National Council of the Churches of Christ in the United States of America. Used by permission. All rights reserved worldwide.

ISBN 978-1-955142-49-6 (print)
ISBN 978-1-955142-50-2 (eBook)

Cover and interior design: Jude May
Cover image © Paul Campbell | iStock images

100 Movements Publishing
An imprint of Movement Leaders Collective
Richmond, Virginia
www.movementleaderscollective.com

*Unless the Lord builds the house,*
*those who build it labor in vain.*
PSALM 127:1

# CONTENTS

Foreword: Danielle Strickland                                      xiii

Introduction: A Quick Read to Set Up the Book                     xvii

1.  IT'S HARD BEING ATLAS                                            1
    *A Burden Never Meant for Us*

2.  THE SHAPING OF LEADERSHIP                                       19
    *Why We Believe What We Believe*

3.  A DIFFERENT ATLAS                                               43
    *Everything Rises and Falls on Headship*

4.  AUTHORITY, WARFARE, AND WEAKNESS                                65
    *Realigning Headship*

5.  HEAD OF A FAMILY                                                91
    *Realigning as a Household of Faith*

6.  FELLOWSHIP OF EQUALS                                           111
    *Realigning through Equality*

7.  UNTAPPED WISDOM                                                145
    *Realigning With the Wisdom of the Older Ones*

8.  RESTRUCTURING AND REHABILITATING
    THE BODY                                                       177
    *Practical Matters and Next Steps*

Acknowledgments                                                    203

# FOREWORD

Danielle Strickland

I'm gonna be honest. I'm struggling to keep my hope alive for the current state of the North American church. I'm exhausted by the seemingly endless revelations of complete moral collapse and what seems to be a genuine systemic flaw that produces people who use their power to protect themselves at the expense of others. I feel like I am banging my head against a wall as I talk with boards across Christian sectors (churches, NGOs, parachurch ministries, seminaries), whose primary impulse is to protect "the brand," even at the cost of truth and the care of its members. What have we become? And how did we get here?

Now, I also know that there are thousands of devoted Jesus-followers—often overlooked and unseen—who lead faith communities beautifully and self-sacrificially. These leaders represent the light, life, and practices of Jesus in glorious, humble, and selfless ways. Persevering and consistently present, they are a witness to the character of God. They are a light in dark times. I'm grateful for them. And I long to be more like them.

I've benefited from the influence of incredibly powerful and gifted leaders who have modeled to me what it looks like to lead like Jesus. I was mentored by a woman who was the world leader of The Salvation Army. She led more than a million members in over 120 countries. She was a beloved leader who could hold stadiums of people spellbound with her preaching and yet still know the names and stories of individual people serving in the back alley behind the stadium. When this wonderful woman retired, she felt the Spirit leading her to spend her final decades working to serve the poor—returning to her original missional calling. If you were homeless, lonely, and cold on the streets in the downtown core of Melbourne, Australia, you could find a warm Salvation Army urban center, with coffee on, welcoming you to a community of Jesus-followers. And the first person you'd meet—the one waiting at the front door—was the former leader of a world movement, who would greet you with a smile, give you a firm handshake (or often a hug), and welcome you home.

That's not all she did; she also lent her authority and influence to empower the whole community and to support other important and credible issues. She regularly called the mayor, met with funders and CEOs of global initiatives, and always advocated for the marginalized. Her witness of faithfulness has always been like a flame burning deeply within my own spirit, reminding me of the kind of leader I'd like to be. There are many more like her. But not nearly enough. And even though they exist, they are almost invisible behind the giant billboard of "successful" and "independent," predominantly male "expert leaders" who are ascending to greatness, triumph, and victory. Those leaders—often called pastors—operate more like kings than priests and lead people into self-ascendancy and grandiose importance, far removed from ordinary people. This is the hierarchy of current church leadership that threatens to undo the entire witness of the church in our culture. And tragically, I believe it is also the greatest threat to the leaders themselves. They get caught in a cycle of self-centering systems, trapped in the moving gears of worldly power, trampled under the weight of responsibility, and end up unseen, unknown, and unloved.

This is the greatest tragedy of our times in the church. We are stuck in systems and mindsets that sound empowering but fuel an oppressive cycle of control and autonomy that drives us through fear, isolates us from others, and serves itself.

What are we to do? How do we get off the hamster wheel of Western church "success" that isn't leading to transformation? When can we start asking the kind of questions that might lead to our mutual flourishing and liberation? What if Catholic social activist Dorothy Day was right when she pinpointed the real problem concerning poverty is not that individuals are stuck in its grip but that we keep bolstering the systems that support and sustain it? Our problems, she said, stem from the dirty, rotten system.[1] And until we get to the heart of the issue—which is our complicity with systems that oppress—we will never really solve the root issues and liberate anyone. This liberation is at the core of this book. What if the problem is not just one leader failing but a whole system of belief and practice that is rooted in a false ideal of what leadership even is? What if the construct of "success" is distorted and needs a transformation? What if the answer is in Christ? What if we took the time to unpack our assumptions and mindsets around church and leadership and allowed the Spirit of Christ to transform not just our practices but our rooted beliefs?

In a world where we emphatically agree that power corrupts, Jesus personified a divine power that didn't. Jesus had absolute power and remained completely untainted by it. That itself is something that should compel us to revisit the divine calling and equipping of the church. To access power, steward it faithfully, and keep giving it away is the work of the church and the essence of the gospel.

I pray this book helps you fall in love with Jesus again. I hope this book disrupts your cultural concepts of leadership and church. I believe these words can be a catalyst to unleash a fresh hunger for divine power—an incorruptible, dynamic energy, freely given for us to freely give away. In this way, we unshackle ourselves from theories, systems, and burdens that wear us down, corrode our faith, and exhaust our resources. Together we can identify the things that steal, kill, and destroy (John 10:10), even if those things have been handed to us as a "Christian principle." We can contend instead for the life-giving abundance of Jesus. This is my greatest hope. I'm believing for the day when every "successful leader" finds themselves as a doorkeeper in the house of the Lord ... welcoming everyone home.

---

[1] See Mark Longhurst, "Creating Space to Listen: How We Choose the New Daily Meditations Theme," The Center for Action and Contemplation, December 14, 2022, https://cac.org/news/creating-space-to-listen-how-we-choose-the-new-daily-meditations-theme/.

# INTRODUCTION

## A Quick Read to Set Up the Book

Most authors write from a burden. Compelled to put words to something we are seeing, or at least something we think we are seeing, we point to significant changes we think need to happen. In 2012, burdened by the leadership culture that had become pervasive in the church, I wrote a book called *UnLeader*. Something was *off*. It was apparent to me that pastors and faith-based leaders—not all, but many—had embraced a leadership system that conflicted with much of what Jesus and the New Testament writers say about leadership. My overarching concern was that, if we continued along this path, not only were many leaders in for a crash, but the church as a whole would be prevented from reaching its potential for fullness in Christ. The reputation of the church and, more importantly, Jesus, was being tarnished.

A couple of years after *UnLeader* came out, I was speaking at a conference in Seattle. During a break between sessions, introducing himself by his first name only, a guy approached me and invited me to eat lunch with him. We walked to a pizza place, and I followed him into a private party room where, to my surprise about eight other guys were waiting for us—none of whom I knew. Then my host came clean. The entire group, himself included, were current or former staff members or elders at Mars Hill Church, the infamous enclave of Mark Driscoll.

The group shared that, after reading *UnLeader*, they had questions and wanted to convene with me about what I had written. I assumed I was in for a debate—but that was far from the case. They told me the book had given them language for what they had been feeling. It had given them theology for issues they had identified in the leadership of Mars Hill that were troubling them. I saw hope in their eyes, but I also sensed dread. Four months later, Mars Hill caved in. And in the years since, a plethora of other well-known pastors and ministries all across the world have followed suit.

Today, more than ten years since *UnLeader* was published, much has been written, podcasted, and discussed regarding the issues and problems of leadership in the church. We have become adept at *naming* the issues plaguing leadership in the church, but I am not convinced we have done enough—or, more importantly, listened to the Lord closely enough—to begin to find a solution. Complaining about darkness helps no one. We need to flip on the light switch if we are going to find our way out and get to where we should be.

My intention for the book you are reading now is to point to some ways we need to reform leadership in the church. By no means do I believe I have all, or even most, of the answers. But I do believe this book contains vital keys to move us in the right direction. And I believe this move starts with shifting leadership onto the shoulders of Jesus, the Head of the church.

We have made Christian leadership into something it was never intended to be. We have made it too hard. Too hard on the shepherds, too hard on staff members, and too hard on the flock. We have also missed out on the strength and vitality the body of Christ has to offer. My intention in the pages ahead is to help you and your church or faith-based organization move toward becoming the beautiful, joyful, Spirit-filled expression of the body of Christ that God intends you to be.

I am writing for church leaders, church planters, and leaders of faith-based organizations who are willing and even desperate to develop a leadership system and structure that eliminates all barriers to the free flow of the life of God in the body of Christ.

You will not find a leadership *model* laid out in this book. Models are not reliable. (Think model homes, fashion models, and model cars.) Models over-promise and under-deliver. They fain perfection but fail in the practicality of real life. What you will find in the pages of this book, however, are *structural components*. Every church, just like every human body, is different in size, shape, and overall makeup. None of us look the same, sound the same, walk the same, or have the same mannerisms. Aren't you glad of that? It is what makes human beings so amazing and wonderful to be around. The body of Christ is like this. Every local expression has a unique size, voice, and way of carrying itself. Our attempts to identify and emulate perfect models have drained our churches of the beauty and gifts the Lord intends them to possess and offer.

Despite our differences, every healthy human body has the same *structure* and *systems*. In the church, our fundamental problem is not abuses in the current leadership system; it is the system itself. We have a *systemic* problem, and it has everything to do with the connection between the Head and the body—the relation between Jesus and his church. My prayer for you is that, as you read this book, the beauty and limitless potential emanating from God's glorious design of the body of Christ and its vital alignment to Jesus as Head will open your imagination to see the awe-inspiring potential of every member set free to fulfill their calling in God's kingdom.

# 1

# IT'S HARD BEING ATLAS

## A Burden Never Meant for Us

*The whole paradigm of solo-heroic leadership assumes that the leader is the smartest and most qualified person to lead in each situation, but the truth is that we is always smarter than me.*

BRYAN D. SIMS

*"They love to sit at the head table at church dinners, basking in the most prominent positions, preening in the radiance of public flattery, receiving honorary degrees, and getting called 'Doctor' and 'Reverend.'*
*"Don't let people do that to you, put you on a pedestal like that. You all have a single Teacher, and you are all classmates. Don't set people up as experts over your life, letting them tell you what to do. Save that authority for God; let him tell you what to do. No one else should carry the title of 'Father'; you have only one Father, and he's in heaven. And don't let people maneuver you into taking charge of them. There is only one Life-Leader for you and them—Christ.*
*"Do you want to stand out? Then step down. Be a servant. If you puff yourself up, you'll get the wind knocked out of you."*

MATTHEW 23:6–12 MSG

One afternoon, I binge-watched a string of *The World's Strongest Man* competition videos. These were not merely big men. They were mountainous specimens, with enormous arms, rock-like shoulders, and bulging thighs. The competitors were tasked with picking up and carrying a variety of heavy items—gigantic boulders, tractor tires, iron chains, and industrial equipment. The athletes vied against one another to determine who could transfer the load of tremendously weighty items from one point to another in the shortest amount of time—as verified by an official competition clock. Their power, will, and stamina were astounding. But by the end of each event, every behemoth was reduced to a quivering mass, bent over or sprawled on their backs, gasping for air, completely fatigued by the weight of their various burdens.

The burden of leadership can feel like that.

## MYTHOLOGICAL LEADERSHIP

Most of us are familiar with Atlas, the mythological Greek figure condemned by Zeus to hold up the heavens. If you have ever been a pastor, at some point you have probably identified with Atlas. Being the leader of a church is often overwhelming. Pastors are expected to be the top in-house theologian, communicator, leadership expert, marriage and parenting sensei, CEO, fundraiser, vision caster, managerial expert, decision-maker, and face of the church. And every day echoes the threatening mantra of "everything rises or falls on leadership." In other words, everything rises or falls on *you*.

No less than the venerable Eugene Peterson, author of *The Message*, struggled as a young church pastor. Peterson's authorized biographer, Winn Collier, shared many years of friendship with Eugene and his wife, Jan. As part of his research, Collier spent countless hours interviewing the couple and was given wide access to Eugene's letters and journals. "Eugene was hung between two competing visions of what it meant to be a pastor," Collier writes. "Preaching from Acts, he saw how clearly everything depended on God. But tossing in bed late at night or poring over endless financial forms whose figures made dark prophecies, it felt as though everything depended on *him*. And he was not sure he was up for the job."[1]

Like the strongman competitors, many pastors are struggling to carry the weight of ministry. A 2021 report from the Barna Group revealed that 38 percent of pastors confided they considered quitting within the previous year. That number jumped to 46 percent of pastors under the age of forty-five; nearly half were seriously contemplating bailing out of the full-time vocation of pastoral leadership. The same report also noted that "many pastors are not faring well in multiple categories of well-being, including relational, spiritual, physical, emotional, vocational and financial."[2]

As a former pastor for over two decades, that report didn't surprise me in the least. My tenure as a senior pastor ended after a ten-year run as the founder of a "successful" evangelical church. I had started as a take-charge, gung-ho, nothing-can-stop-me, thirty-year-old, mulleted church planter. At the end of my run, I was hollow-souled, balding, questioning my calling and ability, and searching for identity. I could see no other option than to quit. I had no more rally-the-troops speeches to offer. No more "vision" to share. No more enthusiasm. No more leadership capacity. And if anyone had handed me one more book on leadership, I would most likely be writing this from prison right now.

The image on the cover of this book shows a guy attempting to be Atlas. No doubt you've seen the more classical images of this Greek mythological figure. Most depictions show a hulking lone figure, stooping, balancing the weight of the heavens on his shoulders.

It's a gross understatement to say that would be a tough job. But just look at him! He appears to be built for such a task. If anyone could

---

[1] Winn Collier, A *Burning in My Bones: The Authorized Biography of Eugene H. Peterson* (Colorado Springs, CO: WaterBrook, 2021), 126.

[2] "38% of U.S. Pastors Have Thought About Quitting Full-Time Ministry in the Past Year," Barna, November 16, 2021, www.barna.com/research/pastors-well-being.

do it, it would be Atlas! But look closer. Atlas is being crushed. Holding the weight of the heavens on his shoulders was a punishment—a task not meant for any one person.

3

You probably didn't become a pastor or church planter because you wanted to carry all the weight. You did not intend to be an Atlas. I'm guessing the dream is, or was, to form a faithful and loving group of Jesus-following people who would bless a local community and enjoy communion on the journey. You may fall into "the dream *was* ..." category. And it may be hard for you to reach back to the simplicity of that place. Not a dream to build something big or make a name for yourself; just a sweet, long obedience in the same direction.[4]

But when we adopt many of today's leadership structures, we are shaped into something Jesus never intended for us. Those structures impose an Atlas-like burden on us. As we will see shortly, today's

---

3    Image credit: "Atlas Sculpture Statue," https://www.needpix.com/photo/1095076/.

4    Friedrich Nietzsche used this phrase in his early twentieth-century book titled *Beyond Good and Evil.*

most-embraced leadership paradigms cast mythological expectations upon "top-level" leaders. From antiquity onward, tribes, clans, and nations have longed for a pedestalled individual to lead them. And despite unavoidable weakness in every human being that has ever drawn a breath, we still believe individual persons can carry and bring about our hoped-for future.

In democratic countries, every election cycle offers candidates who capture the imagination of the masses; men or women we believe will lead us to the promised land. Whether it is a candidate who offers the audacity of hope or one who promises to make America great again, we buy in to one or another. This is not new. Ancient Israel famously demanded that God give them a king despite the Lord already serving as their king and disseminating his leadership through the voices of his chosen prophets, priests, and judges.

> But the thing displeased Samuel when they said, "Give us a king to judge us." And Samuel prayed to the LORD. And the LORD said to Samuel, "Obey the voice of the people in all that they say to you, for they have not rejected you, but they have rejected me from being king over them."
>
> 1 SAMUEL 8:6–7

God gave the people of Israel what they asked for, but he wanted to make it clear that, in doing so, he was acknowledging their rejection of him as their king (v. 7). By declaring, "We must have one man ruling over us," they were saying, "We don't want *you* ruling over us, God. We have a better idea. A better system."

The Lord already had a leadership system in place. It was a structure that kept *him* at the forefront and his counsel, wisdom, and directives accessible to everyone. But Israel wanted a human at the top; someone they could tangibly see and hear. God was invisible, and it took intentional listening to hear his voice. Astoundingly, although Israel had oppressively suffered under the scepter of human rulers, they chose the systems of the fallen world for their leadership blueprint.

## THE SOLO-HEROIC LEADER

At the forefront of continuing leadership failures, we see the concept of what author and leadership professor Bryan Sims calls the *solo-heroic leader*. In his book *Leading Together,* Sims notes, "We've fallen into the trap of believing that only a lone senior leader can be the vision holder. Only s/he knows what is best for the organization they lead."[5] He goes on to say that the Marvel character Iron Man embodies the archetypal solo-heroic leader:

> No doubt you're familiar with the type: the superbly gifted, coura-
> geous, often reckless, arrogant, detached, lone genius. In countless
> scenes throughout the comics and movies, Iron Man needs help but
> prefers to solve the world's biggest problems by himself. Others come
> to his aid, yet he refuses to acknowledge his need for help and insists
> on hoarding the glory for any successes. As a result, others often feel
> small around him. We admire Iron Man's courage and are inspired
> by his genius, but most of us end up feeling sorry for this lonely, self-
> absorbed character.[6]

In perhaps the most widely read leadership texts among pastors, *The 21 Irrefutable Laws of Leadership*, John Maxwell quotes Leroy Eims: "A leader is one who sees more than others see, who sees farther than others see, and who sees before others do."[7] There is no subtlety in those words. The stake in the ground is that the senior leader has *superior* vision. He or she is the go-to seer.

This phenomenon is not limited to large churches. It is prevalent in many small churches as well. In fact, the toll it takes on many men and women in smaller churches is enormous. The present leadership

---

[5] Bryan D. Sims, *Leading Together: The Holy Possibility of Harmony and Synergy in the Face of Change* (Cody: WY, 100 Movements Publishing, 2022), xvii.

[6] Ibid., 15–16.

[7] John C. Maxwell, *The 21 Irrefutable Laws of Leadership: Follow Them and People Will Follow You* (Nashville, TN: Thomas Nelson, 1998), 36.

understanding of the overwhelming majority of our churches has caused too many mere mortals to mistakenly assume the role of Atlas, even though I have little doubt that most pastors never planned to be or do anything less than serve the Lord faithfully from good intentions and hearts.

In her book *Celebrities For Jesus*, Katelyn Beaty writes,

> Many of the fallen Christian leaders we reported on over the years had not started out as celebrities. They had started out in ministry by gaining a following for their accomplishments, creativity, or virtue—the previously explored avenues for fame. They had wanted to serve their community or make a dramatic impact. Almost always, they had started out hoping to make more out of the name of Christ than their own.[8]

We have placed the unbearable weight of leadership on the shoulders of humans. All the while, the Lord declared the government would be on *his* shoulders (Isaiah 9:6).

In *The Starfish and The Spirit*, I shared the following account of a visit I had with a young pastor:

> Meeting at a local coffee shop, Steven, the founding pastor of a church that had grown to around 1,100 members, and I sat down to discuss the young pastor's discontent after over a decade of leading the church he started. "I can't pinpoint what it is I'm feeling," Steven said. "Don't get me wrong. I love our church, and I'm not looking to move on. But I am just so weary of the weight and pace of carrying this thing. Something seems off."
>
> Over the next couple of hours, I asked Steven to give an overview of how day-to-day workflow and responsibilities were

---

[8] Katelyn Beaty, *Celebrities for Jesus: How Personas, Platforms, and Profits Are Hurting the Church* (Grand Rapids, MI: Brazos Press, 2022), 21.

carried out—the way the church was governed and the methods with which accountability and authority were practiced among the staff. Next I had Steven draw the church's organizational structure with the names and titles of those involved. The result was a classic pyramid leadership chart. At one point I spun the sketch 180 degrees. "All that weight is on the point, Steven. You're the point because so much *points* toward you. That's a lot of weight on your shoulders," I said, before steering the conversation to a prophetic promise of the coming Messiah: "For to us a child is born, to us a son is given; and the government shall be upon *his* shoulder, and his name shall be called Wonderful Counselor, Mighty God, Everlasting Father, Prince of Peace" (Isaiah 9:6, emphasis added).

Steven pushed back from the table and sighed deeply, saying, "Wow, that sounds so refreshing and hopeful."

Just imagine the momentous value this familiar verse can bring if we stop limiting it to glittery Christmas cards and cantatas and allow it to shape and inform our leadership approach. It is a promise! The weight of governing rests on the triune Godhead of the Holy Spirit (counselor), Father, and Son (Prince of Peace). The burden of leadership rests there. When we acknowledge it as such, our leadership role opens up to God's counsel, might, and peace. The *government* shall be upon *his* shoulder.[9]

To an overwhelming degree, the underpinning of training for pastors and church leaders has focused on the greatness of an individual at the top. Everything rises and falls on the performance, ability, and traits of one person. We even have seminars and conferences just for senior pastors. And churches of all sizes often place the name of the senior pastor on a sign in front of their buildings.

---

[9]   Lance Ford, Rob Wegner, Alan Hirsch, *The Starfish and The Spirit: Unlocking the Leadership Potential of Churches and Organizations* (Grand Rapids, MI: Zondervan, 2021), 92.

But look at this sketch. While it appears that the solo leader is on the top, spin the image 180 degrees. Our hierarchical structures that seem to have the senior leader at the top, in reality, put them at the bottom—being crushed by the weight of the ministry, like Atlas.

As a young church planter, I asked one of my church-planting heroes what he believed was the most important ingredient for success. He asked if I was ready for the answer. "Yes, what is it?" I asked eagerly. He said two words: *"The guy."* My mentor then listed the vital traits necessary to get the job done: "The guy" must be able to draw a crowd, command a room, make tough decisions, kick people off the bus, raise money, cast a compelling vision, be worthy of respect and even be feared to a degree. He then told me "the guy" must keep a measure of distance between himself and his staff. "You can't be friends with your staff. If you do, they won't respect you."

As I wrote the paragraph above, the front cover of the late Darrin Patrick's widely read book *Church Planter: The Man, The Message, The Mission*, came to mind. It bears the image of a lone, bedraggled man standing in the middle of a wheat field, reaping sickle in hand, with a forlorn expression of absolute exhaustion.[10] The image is meant to convey that it is all about "the guy." We are led to believe there is something heroic about being "the guy"—but it's hard being Atlas.

## LONELY AT THE TOP

The summer after tenth grade, I worked for my Uncle Charley. He had a good sense of humor, but when it was time for work, he was as rough as a stucco bathtub. When he wanted something done, he expected it to be accomplished as soon as the words left his mouth. And oh, what words he had. They were as colorful as a Sherwin-Williams paint catalog. Charley was a World War II veteran who had received the Purple Heart for being shot in combat. He grew up in the tiny town of Era, Texas, and it was there that he eventually took over my maternal grandfather's water well business.

The summer I worked for him just so happened to be the year of fifty-two straight days of 100-degree-plus weather—a record for Texas at the time. The work was hellishly hot and revolved around heavy, grease-laden machinery. That summer I came to understand the phrase, "Rode hard and put up wet." He pushed me harder than I have ever been pushed.

---

[10] Darrin Patrick, *Church Planter: The Man, The Message, The Mission* (Wheaton, IL: Crossway, 2010).

The drilling rig was known as a "spudder." Instead of having a modern rotary bit, this rig's drill bit was a 15-foot solid steel three-inch shaft, suspended by a cable over a pulley at the top of a 40-foot mast. The drill bit would rise about 20 feet and drop, pounding the earth, over and over. *Bam, bam, bam.* One day, the cable jumped off the pulley at the top of the mast. Charley cussed and shut the rig down. "How are you going to fix that?" I asked. "I'm not," he shouted back, "You are." He told me to climb up and reset the cable. I was just sixteen years old and had a lot to live for. I had a sparkling '76 Oldsmobile Cutlass, filled with eight-track tapes, a girlfriend, and weekend plans. The last thing I wanted to do was climb up that blazing hot rig. But it wasn't the heat I was thinking about. It was the height. The only other option was to have my emerging manhood eviscerated by Charley's verbal paint pallet, so up I went. When I got to the top of the mast, I couldn't lift the cable up and over the pulley. With all my might, and all my grunting, I just could not quite get it in place. I could hear Charley screaming at me from down below. But there was no getting it done. I finally decided to give up, descend the mast, and take my medicine from Charley. He would have to come up with a Plan B. Little did I know he was already implementing it.

As I made the first move downward, I felt the mast shake. It swayed a bit. "What the ...," I muttered. Looking below, I saw Charley coming up the mast. It quickly dawned on me that there was only enough space for one guy at the top. *Where does he think he is going?* As I held on for dear life, I could hear Charley cursing a blue streak, getting louder as he got closer. I learned things about my ancestry and personal species I didn't know before as he made his way up. "Get your (foul/filth/foul/filth) ____ out of the (foul/filth/foul/filth) ____ing way!" Charley yelled, as his cowboy hat slammed into my Wrangler jeans' back pockets. He wasn't stopping, and there was no place for me to go. I was already at the top. By this time, the mast was steadily swaying back and forth. My only choice for survival was to go up and over the pulley and cling for dear life to the other side of the mast. Charley and I managed to get the cable in place, and once we were back on the ground, he lit a cigarette, pushed his cowboy hat up from his forehead, and said, "Now, you're a driller." *Nope,* I thought to myself, *I am a future former driller.*

I learned two things that day. First, I didn't want to be in that business. Second, being on top was perilous.

Pastors and leaders talk all the time about how lonely it is "at the top"—and it can sometimes seem like a humble brag. But it is indeed a real and serious issue. Researchers regularly publish reports that reveal the lonely state of pastors:

> 55 percent [of pastors] say being in pastoral ministry makes them feel lonely at times. ... The study found that 18 percent of pastors have more than 10 close friends in their congregation. Sixteen percent have six to 10, 38 percent have three to five, 10 percent have two and 4 percent have one. Twelve percent of pastors have no close friends in their congregation.[11]

> 61% of pastors are lonely and have few close friends.[12]

> The Barna survey [showed] almost half of pastors are considering quitting the ministry. Nearly half of that group cites loneliness and isolation as part of the problem.[13]

Pastor and author Tom Nelson writes,

> After I had finished speaking to a group of pastors on the dangers of pastoral isolation, a pastor approached me with droplets of tears on his face. His surfacing emotion and his transparent words

[11] David Roach, "Poll: Many pastors feel lonely, discouraged," *Baptist Press*, October 20, 2011, https://www.baptistpress.com/resource-library/news/poll-many-pastors-feel-lonely-discouraged/.

[12] Charles Stone, "5 reasons pastors lack friends," *Biblical Leadership*, February 14, 2021, https://www.biblicalleadership.com/blogs/5-reasons-why-pastors-lack-friends/.

[13] Richard Rose, "Rose: Lonely pastors and the rest of us, too," *Amarillo Globe-News*, accessed April 15, 2023, https://www.amarillo.com/story/opinion/2022/05/29/richard-rose-lonely-pastors-and-rest-us-too/9943707002/.

immediately connected us at the heart level. Standing before me was a seasoned pastor who had faithfully served a local church for almost thirty years. Yet at the overwhelming realization, he could no longer ignore his own isolation. As I put my arms around him, words of heartache tumbled out of his weary soul. "For thirty years, I have done this alone, keeping my arm's distance from others. I am going to wither and die without community."[14]

Unfortunately, the advice or antidote for leadership loneliness given to senior pastors is usually to find some other senior-pastor friends to hang out with on a regular basis. This solution is akin to the Alcoholics Anonymous dictum credited to founder Bill Wilson: "I needed another alcoholic." The idea is that no one else can understand what the senior leader goes through besides another senior leader. But rarely considered is whether we should be *senior* leaders in the first place. Is *anyone* intended to be *the guy* (or *the gal*) in Jesus' leadership construct?

When Jesus declared, "It shall not be so among you" (Matthew 20:26), he was countering the culture of the day, where the rulers of the Gentiles lorded it over them. In doing so, Jesus was setting up the ground rules and agreement between himself and those who would represent his name and ways. For those of us who claim to have entered into this agreement, we are declaring we will turn our backs on the way the world's systems fashion leadership. We are taking an oath, "It will not be so among us. We will refuse to use the tactics, processes, and systems that allow any one person to dominate another. We will not use force against one another. We will turn our backs on schemes and policies that suppress truth in order to protect our reputations. We will not elevate ourselves above our brothers or sisters in Christ. We will not leverage rank and title through fear and carnal intimidation. We will refuse to ascend the ladder of status but instead take a knee, with

---

[14] Tom Nelson, *The Flourishing Pastor: Recovering the Lost Art of Shepherd Leadership* (Downers Grove, IL: InterVarsity Press, 2021), location 358, Kindle.

bowl and towel in hand, to wash one another's feet—not in ceremonial rituals but in the perpetual role of servant."

## IT'S THE SYSTEM, STUPID

Of all the great men and women throughout biblical history, the Lord called just one person a "man after [my] heart" (Acts 13:22). And yet that man, King David, who was so in tune with the intimacies of the Spirit of God that he penned most of the psalms, could not handle power. He abused his position in the most heinous of ways. If David couldn't handle kingly autonomy, what makes us think we can?

When we hear of the latest fallen pastor or leader of a faith-based institution, our hearts sink. And we have witnessed it so frequently that we wonder, *Who's next?* Christian leadership scandals have been front-page news, particularly since the 1980s televangelist train wrecks. Who can forget the image of Jimmy Swaggart tearfully admitting, "I have sinned," only to do the same thing again in short order?[15] Or Jim Bakker, crying as federal agents led him away in handcuffs for mail and wire fraud?[16] Years later, Ted Haggard, a mega-church pastor and president of the National Association of Evangelicals, was ousted in a scandal of illicit sex and illegal drug use.[17] Those downfalls were marked by sexual promiscuity, but over the past decade, a multitude of pastors from the largest of evangelical churches, ministries, and institutions have gone down in flames amid verified accusations of bullying, pride, and abuse of authority. The

---

[15] Wayne King, "Swaggart Says He Has Sinned; Will Step Down," *The New York Times*, February 22, 1988, https://www.nytimes.com/1988/02/22/us/swaggart-says-he-has-sinned-will-step-down.html.

[16] "Televangelist Jim Bakker Is Indicted On Federal Charges," *The History Channel*, November 13, 2009, https://www.history.com/this-day-in-history/jim-bakker-is-indicted-on-federal-charges.

[17] Eric Whitney, "Haggard Admits Buying Drugs, Getting Massage," *NPR*, November 3, 2006, https://www.npr.org/2006/11/03/6430392/haggard-admits-buying-drugs-getting-massage.

scandals used to be mostly about personal failings, but more and more systemic failures are being uncovered.

Sadly, the most influential pastors in recent times who have been dismissed for abuse of authority are Bill Hybels, Mark Driscoll, and Brian Houston.[18] Leading large networks and associations, they have been some of the most significant voices in church leadership over the past two to three decades. When leaders such as these are exposed, it doesn't mean their errors suddenly cease. Instead, the systems and structures perpetuated by such powerful men, under the mantra of *leadership*, have had an incalculable impact on the thinking and methods of thousands of pastors and church planters via the conferences, books, and direct training they offered.

In the organizations of the three leaders mentioned above, a cadre of other top-level leaders went down for similar reasons. If we were to do an autopsy on their leadership body, we would have to conclude that something toxic in their leadership circulatory system caused their demise. It was not a singular misstep or mistake that brought them down. When I think of these leadership transgressions, I'm reminded of the phrase coined by Bill Clinton's 1992 presidential campaign strategist James Carville. He said, "It's the economy, stupid." However, in relation to church leadership, I believe, "It's the system, stupid."

The intent of this book is not to pile on or disparage individuals. Yet it seems we are not learning much from what continues to happen. The familiar adage, "Power corrupts, and absolute power corrupts absolutely" should be an adequate reminder.[19] The time has come for us to ask if the system of leadership we have unwittingly adopted and given ourselves to has gotten us to this place. In too many cases,

---

[18] Tyler Huckabee, "Brian Houston and the End of the Celebrity Pastor," *Relevant*, March 28, 2022, https://relevantmagazine.com/faith/church/brian-houston-and-the-end-of-the-celebrity-pastor/.

[19] A saying attributed to nineteenth-century British politician Lord John Dalberg Acton.

we have been convinced that church leadership rises and falls on the individual leader and the structures that keep them in power.

But putting individual leaders on the pedestal of solo leadership does not form them into the image of Christ. And if those individual leaders refuse to turn from worldly leadership structures that do not reflect Jesus, then they must be called out.

It is a hard thing to point out individuals by name who are brothers and sisters in Christ. But we are actually commanded to do so. And the writers of the epistles did it.

> If anyone falls into sin, call that person on the carpet. Those who are inclined that way will know right off they can't get by with it. God and Jesus and angels all back me up in these instructions. Carry them out without favoritism, without taking sides. Don't appoint people to church leadership positions too hastily. If a person is involved in some serious sins, you don't want to become an unwitting accomplice. In any event, keep a close check on yourself. And don't worry too much about what the critics will say.
>
> 1 TIMOTHY 5:20–23 MSG

- Paul calls out Cephas (Peter) by name and shares what happened (Galatians 2:11).
- John calls out Diotrephes by name for liking to place himself first (3 John 1:9–10).
- Paul names Hymenaeus and Alexander as blasphemers (1 Timothy 1:20).
- Paul calls out Phygelus and Hermogenes for abandonment (2 Timothy 1:15).
- Paul calls out Demas for loving the world and abandonment (2 Timothy 4:10).

In just the past few years, as a growing number of influential leaders have been accused of leadership abuse, many published reports and articles as well as podcasts have emerged, calling such men out by name. And while these leaders need to be called out, if we only point the finger at them, and not the systems that formed them, we are doomed to continue in our broken church-leadership cycles.

The myth of Atlas is a warning to us, and we have assumed his role at our own peril and the peril of countless churches, pastors, and the families of pastors. We have taken the Lord's name in vain, not by using his name as a curse word but by doing something in the Lord's name that he explicitly commanded us not to do. Worse yet, we have brought shame and disdain upon the Lord's name in the eyes of the watching world, who now see the Lord's name as a curse. In the words of the apostle Paul, we have claimed to build in the name of the Lord but instead have built with "wood, hay, [and] straw" (1 Corinthians 3:12). And, as Paul said, "Their work will be shown for what it is, because the Day will bring it to light. It will be revealed with fire, and the fire will test the quality of each person's work" (1 Corinthians 3:13–14 NIV).

What is the ultimate end of such people? The answer is not for us to judge, but the scripture above continues with words of eternal hope: "If it is burned up, the builder will suffer loss but yet will be saved—even though only as one escaping through the flames" (1 Corinthians 3:15 NIV).

Atlas. A Greek tragedy has become a modern-day reality, played out not on the stages of theater but in the church of Jesus Christ. So, how did we get here?

## For Teams to Process

- In what ways might contemporary leadership concepts be shaping us into something we did not originally aspire to?

- How have our individual aspirations for accomplishment, creativity, or virtue influenced the culture of leadership within our team?
- How is the concept of the "solo-heroic leader" present in our leadership culture?
- In what ways have we unintentionally placed an overwhelming burden of leadership on individual pastors, rather than fostering a collective approach?
- How has the current top-down leadership approach affected our team's effectiveness and well-being? What are some risks and pitfalls we should be aware of?
- Reflecting on the statistics mentioned in this chapter, how do we perceive the level of loneliness and lack of community within our own team? Are there some among us who feel isolated or disconnected?
- What alternatives or solutions should be considered to address leadership loneliness and foster community among our team?

# 2

# THE SHAPING OF LEADERSHIP

## Why We Believe What We Believe

*The most difficult subjects can be explained to the most slow-witted man if he has not formed any idea of them already; but the simplest thing cannot be made clear to the most intelligent man if he is firmly persuaded that he knows already, without a shadow of doubt, what is laid before him.*

LEO TOLSTOY

I've been entrenched in leadership since I was a peach-fuzzed, wide-eyed Bible college student. During those years—the mid-1980s—there was plenty of big hair, *Miami-Vice* pastel, and synthesized music filling the fledgling MTV airwaves. A new trend had emerged in the evangelical church as well that would become much more than a short-lived fad. The focus on *leadership* among pastors was in its early stages, but it was growing like a tidal wave. The tsunami of church leadership books, conferences, and articles was still a few years off; but coming it was. The church-growth movement of the 1970s was an earthquake, and it set a tidal wave in motion. When it hit the shores of the Western church, what the foaming waves didn't cover, the rolling waters seeped into.

Leadership became *the* thing, and it oozed into every crevice of evangelical churchdom. In 1980, in response to the growing market demand, *Christianity Today* launched *Leadership Journal*—a spinoff publication aimed at satisfying pastors' desires for cutting-edge (another very '80s term) expertise in their field of work. The periodical was a smash hit. In the fourth volume, *Christianity Today* President Harold Myra wrote:

> Frankly, it's been a wild—but invigorating—ride. We thought we were birthing a canary, but out came this huge eagle. Here we are, clutching its talons as it flies up and up to new vistas, whereas we thought by now we'd be watching a polite little yellow thing twittering in its cage. Our original *Leadership* plans were for 5000 circulation and modest beginnings. But testing and research showed intense need and interest. We soon knew we had to give it our best shot—extensive editorial work, full-time staff, major promotions ... launching circulation to 60,000 this first year.[1]

By the mid-1990s it was "leadership game on." Pastors had developed an insatiable appetite for the subject. Magazines such as *Fast Company*, *Business Monthly*, and *Harvard Business Review* benefitted as a new constituency of subscribers came on board—pastors. Leadership conferences replaced camp meetings and prayer gatherings, while leadership seminars drove "revival" meetings into near extinction. "Give me that old-time religion" became "Give me those leadership best practices." And over the last thirty-plus years, leadership has grown into an all-consuming topic among ministers. Walk into a typical pastor's office or study, and you will see bookshelves filled with a mix of texts on leadership expertise, organizational excellence, and biographies of legendary business gurus and political heads.

The change in focus—dare I say, obsession—happened relatively quickly. Just a decade or so before the leadership outbreak, church leaders weren't called "church leaders"; they were called "pastors," "shepherds," "ministers." *Servants*. Those who served churches

---

[1]  Harold L. Myra, "A Message from the Publisher: October 01, 1980," *Christianity Today*, https://www.christianitytoday.com/pastors/1980/fall/80l4122.html.

didn't view themselves as CEOs and executives; they identified with fishermen-turned-followers of a Nazarene carpenter who made disciples out of everyday people in the shadow of temple power and the powerful men who ruled in the name of God.

How did we get here?

## LEADERSHIP BIAS

In the New Testament, a quick word search in the ESV finds "disciple" used around 260 times, while the word "leader" is mentioned only six times. That is a 43-to-1 ratio! Additionally, any student of Jesus and the writings of the apostle Paul will be familiar with the frequent use of the term "servant." Though it has effectually lost its original meaning, the word "minister" literally means *servant*. Out of curiosity, I once searched Amazon for books with the query "Christian leadership," and it produced over thirty thousand hits. I followed that search with "Christian serving," and the results were around three thousand—a 10-to-1 ratio. This is not empirical data, but at the very least, it should give some indication of what is grabbing our attention. I certainly know I've never heard of a church servantship conference. Have you?

There should be no argument that leadership has become a dominant influence in the minds of pastors. But I don't believe that many church leaders have dug deeply into understanding the foundations of the subject we have been convinced "everything rises or falls" upon. Nothing is more important than who and what we allow our thinking to be influenced by. As the proverb says, "As [one] thinks in his heart, so is he" (Proverbs 23:7 NKJV). What we give our time, attention, and energy to determines our priorities. It is therefore imperative that we give ourselves to the right things.

Our bookshelves hold our most popular texts on leadership, and we have attended more seminars and conferences on the subject than we can count. But few leaders really know the root sources of the content. There are some questions worth asking: "Why do I think the way I do about leadership? Where did this thinking come from, and why does it matter? Did I believe it and pass it along because someone who wrote a lot of popular books, grew a big church, or leads a large institution says it is the key to success? Am I being led and fed from the Lord at the leadership table I so often sit down to?" I hope you agree these questions are indeed worth asking and getting answers to.

Words are important. The study of linguistics reveals not only how words shape people but also how they shape the people of the future. To fail to get our heads around as important a word as "leadership" has enormous consequences. We need to understand the word and why it means what it does to us today. We need to test the term and discover the ways it is helpful and the ways it can be harmful.

To put it another way, we need to dig down to the roots of our own leadership paradigms. If "everything rises or falls on leadership," it is worth examining why we think the way we do about leadership in the first place. It is incumbent on us to earnestly seek the answers to these questions because those answers will reveal whether you and I are thinking with the mind of Christ or the mind of worldly power, pursuits, and imagination—which Paul calls folly (1 Corinthians 3:19). We must understand the source of our building materials.

## STICK TO THE CODEBOOK

My wife, Sherri, and I have built two houses over the years. When I say that I am often asked, "So, you mean you *had* the houses built for you?" No. We built them with our own hands. Sherri designed the house we currently live in, and my son and I built it, before she took over the finishes such as tiling, drywall texturing, and painting. We wanted this house to feature old timber beams, so I did a lot of searching across the country before finding just the right materials. We procured hand-hewn timbers from an 1870s Pennsylvanian property. They are each a work of art. The largest was probably from trees that were at least a hundred years old before being felled by the ax of a pioneer who then painstakingly hewed and scraped the tree into a squared-off timber. I marvel every time I look at them.

A certified engineer did the proper calculations for the roof load; and then my son, father-in-law, brother-in-law, and I spent three days with an extended forklift, putting the framework together.

Our location was in Florida, a place I had never lived before. And there was quite a learning curve. The house had to be built according to the Florida hurricane code. Along with the certification of the engineer, every single item I used to construct the house had to bear an approved code number, and I had to verify to the inspector that I had used approved materials. I was constantly having to go back to construction manuals because we were employing different methods than I had ever used before. It would have been much easier, and I could have finished the house much more quickly if I had built it according to my standards. I was constantly shaking my head at the extra effort I was required to put in because of that *stupid* code.

A year and a half later, the structure was tested severely as Hurricane Michael, a Category 5 beast, hit us dead center. We rode out the storm as it packed 140-mph sustained winds for nearly five hours. Over the din of the raging wind, I prayed and paced hour after hour, looking up at the tons of timbers overhead, pleading for the Lord to keep them from crashing down on top of us. When the wind finally slowed enough for us to go outside, destruction was everywhere. More than four hundred trees on our property were leveled. I could barely bring myself to look at the house we had worked so hard to build. But as I crawled across the thicket of broken trees and looked back at our home, sweet relief came. The house had held its ground. It didn't even creak during the onslaught. There were absolutely no cracks in the drywall anywhere. And the metal roof was intact. To say the least, we were happy we chose the right materials, the right engineer, and the proper construction methods.

Most of all, I was happy for the code that was such a hassle. At that moment, I came to love that code book. Despite my skills and "better" ideas, I know if we had not adhered to the specifications of the code, the house would not have fared so well. Worse yet, my family may have perished. As I surveyed our area, it was clear which houses had been built before the hurricane codes and which had been built after. All around us, homes were uninhabitable or completely flattened.

When building anything in the name of the Lord, the apostle Paul gave us a stern admonition:

> By the grace God has given me, I laid a foundation as a wise builder, and someone else is building on it. But each one should build with care. For no one can lay any foundation other than the one already laid, which is Jesus Christ. If anyone builds on this foundation using gold, silver, costly stones, wood, hay or straw, their work will be shown for what it is, because the Day will bring it to light. It will be revealed with fire, and the fire will test the quality of each person's work. If what has been built survives, the builder will receive a reward. If it is burned up, the builder will suffer loss but yet will be saved—even though only as one escaping through the flames.
>
> Don't you know that you yourselves are God's temple and that God's Spirit dwells in your midst? If anyone destroys God's temple, God will destroy that person; for God's temple is sacred, and you together are that temple.
>
> Do not deceive yourselves. If any of you think you are wise by the standards of this age, you should become "fools" so that you may become wise. For the wisdom of this world is foolishness in God's sight. As it is written: "He catches the wise in their craftiness"; and again, "The Lord knows that the thoughts of the wise are futile."
>
> 1 CORINTHIANS 3:10–20 NIV

As I mentioned earlier, I've been in vocational ministry since I was a pup. Through the years, there were things I read and heard from the most renowned authors and pastors on issues around leadership that sounded brilliant—yet seemed to cut against the grain of what Jesus and the New Testament writers espoused. Some of it was helpful, but a lot of it conflicted with the character of Jesus and instructions from the epistles. Often, I would read a leadership book and would say to myself, "But Jesus said ..." or "That doesn't seem to jibe with Ephesians, where it is written ..."

A lot of the leadership methods and materials clashed with *the* Codebook. But I just went along with it. I attended all the best leadership conferences and became well acquainted with my UPS guy who handed me book deliveries weekly from a little upstart internet bookseller called amazon.com. Despite the "check" in my spirit, I went along with the flow because no one else seemed to question what these experts were saying. And almost all the leaders I admired were doing it this way, so surely there was nothing to be concerned about.

But some of the actions of church leaders I witnessed were out of sync with the ethos and ethics of the kingdom of heaven. I also personally experienced domineering treatment and leadership practices that I knew opposed Scripture and the character of Jesus himself. I could not shake off what I kept seeing in the Codebook of the Master Carpenter. I was compelled to dig deeper. *What are we doing in all of this, and how did we get here?* I wondered. The conundrum pushed me to search for answers.

To thoughtlessly parrot the axiom "everything rises or falls on leadership" is not a good starting place because it fails to ask what leadership *is* in the first place. Most importantly, it ignores how Jesus and the writers of the New Testament defined proper, kingdom-based leadership. Is it possible that contemporary Christian leadership is based on something that is not actually *Christ*-ian?

You have probably heard of or even used online tools such as ancestry.com, 23andme.com, or myheritage.com. These powerful genealogy platforms help individuals trace their personal heritage. Let's do a bit of that type of research into our leadership ancestry. Let's check out our "church leadership" heritage.

## THE ROOTS OF OUR LEADERSHIP PARADIGMS

This chapter could easily be an entire book. I am doing my best to condense at least fifteen years of research into what I consider the most important points. But if you are inclined to dig further into the roots of our leadership paradigms, let me recommend two of the most helpful books I have found. Among other works, Joseph Rost's *Leadership for The Twenty-First Century* and Robert (Bobby) Clinton's *A Short History of Leadership Theory* both provide solid surveys on the shifts in leadership theory.[2] Clinton cites just shy of one hundred books and articles, and Rost references close to six hundred publications. The latter's book serves as a virtual catalog for thorough research of leadership theory from the mid-1800s up to 1991 when it was published. In the next few pages, I will quote some material and paraphrase other portions from these two excellent works.

As Paul warned in the passage above from 1 Corinthians, when we build on the foundation of Jesus and his kingdom by using worldly materials, we enter into folly. What we build doesn't pass the code. We think we are wise but are acting like fools. In fact, when we build using worldly materials, we are not only in danger of building structures that could collapse, but we are also in danger of replacing Jesus as the foundation.

So, let's look at the roots of our leadership paradigms. The next few pages may seem dense and academic, but hang with me. I'm convinced it is worth the brainpower to get where we are headed in this study. As we proceed, keep in mind that I am not declaring *all* leadership is tainted. What I am suggesting is that some of the material and methods conflict with the ways of Jesus and the New Testament writers. We need it *all* to meet the standards of the Codebook.

The subject of leadership has erupted into a $50 billion industry, but the modern concept of leadership is a relatively new idea. As I reverse-engineered the term, I opened my 1950s edition of *The Oxford Universal Dictionary*.[3] It is big enough to be a boat anchor, so I expected to find some great information on the subject. I was in for a surprise.

---

[2] Joseph C. Rost, *Leadership for the Twenty-First Century* (Altadena, CA: Praeger, 1993); Dr. J. Robert Clinton, *Leadership Series: A Short History of Leadership Theory* (Barnabas Publishers, 1992).

[3] First published in 1933 as *The Shorter Oxford English Dictionary*.

What I found was not much at all. I might as well have been opening Al Capone's empty vault. The word "leadership" was barely present—mentioned only in a single brief sentence as part of the definition of the word "leader." I found that shocking. Just seventy years ago, arguably the most-respected English dictionary available had virtually nothing to say about leadership.

Rost says the earliest dictionaries he discovered (from the early fifteenth century) did not even include the word "lead." He came upon a couple of volumes that defined the word "leader" as "one that leads; captain, commander; one who goes first; and one at the head of a party or faction."[4] Rost comments that the word "*leadership* was not defined, giving us the first solid evidence that it was a word English-speaking people did not use in the middle of the eighteenth century."[5] He further points to George Crabb's 1839 book, which sheds light on the connotations of the word "lead" at that time by comparing the words "lead," "conduct," and "guide":

> These terms are all employed to denote the influence which one person has over the movements or actions of another; but the first implies nothing more than personal presence and direction or going before, the last two convey also the idea of superior intelligence. ... In the literal sense it is the hand that *leads*, the head that *conducts*, and the eye that *guides*; one *leads* an infant; *conducts* a person to a given spot; and *guides* a traveller.[6]

Rost alarmingly notes that in Noah Webster's 1828 text, *An American Dictionary of the English Language*, the definition of the word "lead" says: "to draw, entice, allure; to induce, prevail on, influence; to pass, spend, that is draw out; to exercise dominion." He points out that, "The

---

[4] Rost, *Leadership for the Twenty-First Century*, 38.

[5] Ibid., 39.

[6] George Crabb, *English Synonyms, with Copious Illustrations and Explanations, Drawn from the Best Writers* (New York, NY: Harper, 1839), 191.

words *influence* and *exercise dominion* were used for the first time to define the concept of leading."[7]

If the phrase "exercise dominion" rings a bell, it is because that is the very phrase used by Jesus as he rebuked his disciples for their aspirations of leadership, power, and status:

> But Jesus called them unto him, and said, Ye know that the princes of the Gentiles *exercise dominion* over them, and they that are great exercise authority upon them. But it shall not be so among you: but whosoever will be great among you, let him be your minister; And whosoever will be chief among you, let him be your servant: Even as the Son of man came not to be ministered unto, but to minister, and to give his life a ransom for many.
>
> MATTHEW 20:25–28 KJV (EMPHASIS MINE)

So, Webster defined leading as doing the very thing Jesus commands us *not* to do. Very sobering.

## Definitions Through the Decades

From 1900 to 1929, an emphasis on control and centralization of power was pervasive in definitions of leadership.[8] A key presenter at a 1927 conference on leadership defined leadership as "the ability to impress the will of the leader on those led and induce obedience, respect, loyalty, and cooperation."[9] The last part of this definition is particularly problematic. This is where the notion begins to surface that good leaders demand obedience and gather followers of themselves.

Despite disciplined scholarly research, including an extensive survey of rare books, Rost said he found no books on leadership published until the 1930s. At that time, however, the idea of group

---

[7] Rost, *Leadership for the Twenty-First Century*, 39.

[8] Ibid, 47.

[9] B. V. Moore, "The May conference on leadership," *Personnel Journal*, 6, 1927, 124.

leadership emerged—the concept of leadership is not contained in any particular individual but as an *effect* upon group interaction. Sociologist E. S. Bogardus wrote, "Leadership is personality in action under group conditions ... It is interaction between specific traits of one person and other traits of the many, in such a way that the course of action of the many is changed by the one."[10] In his 1935 book *Leadership or Domination*, Paul Pigors wrote, "Leadership is a process of mutual stimulation which by successful interplay of relevant difference, controls human energy in the pursuit of a common cause."[11]

A bevy of authors began to promote a group-leadership paradigm in the 1940s. Rost cites Edward Reuter, Norman Copeland, and Ralph Davis, among others. Reuter, author of *Handbook of Sociology*, wrote, "Leadership is the result of an ability to persuade or direct men, apart from the prestige or power that comes from office or other external circumstances."[12] Along the same lines, Copeland, author of *Psychology and the Soldier*, said, "Leadership ... is the art of influencing a body of people by persuasion or example to follow a line of action. It must never be confused with *drivership*—to coin a word—which is the art of compelling a body of people by intimidation or force to follow a line of action."[13] And Davis, author of *The Fundamentals of Top Management*, defined leadership as "the principle dynamic force that stimulates, motivates, and coordinates the organization in the accomplishment of its objectives."[14] These ideas are sound and satisfy the Jesus code. At this point, there appeared to be a blip on the leadership radar that called for less dominating leadership, but it would fade away before resurfacing a few decades later with voices such as Robert Greenleaf, widely known as the father of "servant leadership."

---

[10]  E. S. Bogardus, *Leaders and Leadership* (New York, NY: Appleton-Century, 1934), 3.

[11]  Paul Â. Pigors, *Leadership or Domination* (Boston, MA: Houghton Mifflin Company, 1935), 16.

[12]  Edward Byron Reuter, *Handbook of Sociology* (Hinsdale, IL: The Dryden Press, 1941), 133.

[13]  Norman Copeland, *Psychology and the Soldier: The Art of Leadership* (Quantico, VA: Military Service Publications, 1942), 77.

[14]  Ralph Currier Davis, *The Fundamentals of Top Management* (New York, NY: Harper & Row, 1942), 27.

Group theory and the important elements of interconnectivity continued to be studied well into the 1950s. Rost quotes several leadership scholars of the time who viewed the essence of leadership as being relational. Professors Andrew Halpin, Janet Bieri, and Benjamin Winer wrote that leadership is "the behavior of an individual when he is directing the activities of a group toward shared goals."[15]

In the 1960s, a focus on effective behavioral traits weighed heavily in shaping leadership definitions. Noted sociologist Melvin Seeman perceived leadership as "acts by persons which influence other persons in a shared direction."[16] Boston College professor of sociology, Ritchie Lowry, wrote "Leadership is the ability (and potential) to influence the decisions and actions of others (followers) and therefore to exercise power over the decision-making process of community life."[17] These definitions are helpful in understanding the thinking during this era.

Arguably the most dominant leadership text at this point was *The Effective Executive* by leadership guru Peter Drucker.[18] His work would shape and influence leaders in an immeasurable way, including the founder of Leadership Network, Bob Buford, who considered Drucker his mentor. Leadership Network heavily influenced the paradigms of a vast number of pastors from the 1990s onward.

Between 1965 and 1990, almost all dictionaries defined leadership as (1) the office or position of a leader and (2) the ability to lead.[19] Space doesn't allow us to cover Rost's thorough research, but he gives an extensive overview of dictionary treatments of the word "leadership" through 1979; and a summary of his conclusions are:

---

[15] Andrew Halpin, Janet Bieri, and Ben Winer, "The Leadership Ideology of Aircraft Commanders," *Journal of Applied Psychology* 39, no. 2 (April 1955): 82–84.

[16] Melvin Seeman, *Social Status and Leadership: The Case of the School Executive* (Columbus: Bureau of Educational Research and Service, Ohio State University, 1960), 127.

[17] Ritchie P. Lowry, *Who's Running This Town?: Community Leadership and Social Change* (New York, NY: Harper & Row, 1965), 8.

[18] Peter Drucker, *The Effective Executive* (New York, NY: Harper & Row, 1966).

[19] Rost, *Leadership for the Twenty-First Century*, 42.

- Leadership only emerged as a popular term after 1900 and still lacked the connotations the word holds today.
- Leadership, as we conceptualize it today, is a twentieth-century notion.
- Dictionary definitions lack depth and offer little help in understanding the concept of leadership beyond "the ability to lead."
- Leadership and management, as defined by dictionaries, are basically synonymous. "Every dictionary since the turn of the [twentieth] century has defined leadership as 'the position or office of a leader,' indicating that leadership involves little more than occupying a position of management or administration."[20]

As noted earlier, the word "leadership" has no definition in some notable English dictionaries prior to the twentieth century and only scant definitions in the few others. Rost could only find the word used in three written texts prior to the 1900s. And Webster's 1915 edition had no definition of the word whatsoever! Let that sink in. Just over a century ago, the most widely trusted English dictionary did not even consider leadership significant enough to mention it. Ralph Stogdill achieved international recognition for his extensive research and writings on leadership and organizations, serving as a distinguished Professor Emeritus of Management Science and Psychology at Ohio State University. He says, "The Oxford English Dictionary (1933) notes the appearance of the word 'leader' in the English language as early as the year 1300. However, the word 'leadership' did not appear until the first half of the nineteenth century in writings about political influence and control of British Parliament."[21]

To summarize so far, the issue or idea of leadership as we know it today is a nascent concept. If it were a person, it would be an infant in diapers! This should give us serious pause. The church is over two

---

[20] Ibid., 43.

[21] Ralph Melvin Stogdill, *Stogdill's Handbook of Leadership: A Survey of Theory and Research*, Revised and Expanded edition, edited by Bernard M. Bass (New York, NY: Free Press, 1981), 7.

thousand years old, but most of the principles we apply today have arisen in the last fifty years.

## Eras of Leadership Theory

Historians call the early era of leadership dogma the age of "Great Man Theory." This theory emerged in the nineteenth century and is attributed to British historian and philosopher Thomas Carlyle, who said, "The history of the world is the biography of great men." Great Man Theory was prevalent from about 1840 to 1900, but the overtones remain today. Not limited to the fields of politics and business, it has fed the celebrity culture of Christian leaders, which continues to produce scandalous results.

Simply stated, this theory suggests that exceptional leaders are born, not made. Such leaders are the ones who come into the world with the "it" factor. They possess innate qualities, attributes, and charisma in their very nature that are beyond what most others can attain. Men and women of this ilk, according to the theory, possess degrees of intuition, intelligence, will, and courage to take action that can't be taught or learned. You either have it or you don't. The early adherents of Great Man Theory pointed to icons such as Teddy Roosevelt, Andrew Carnegie, and Abraham Lincoln. Contemporary democrats may think of Barack Obama while republicans may think of Donald Trump. Great Man Theory placed its hope for noteworthy leadership in one rare and outstanding individual.

Eventually, as Bobby Clinton notes, "The study of leadership shaded over from just the study of Great Men into a search for the qualities commonly evinced in the lives of Great Men."[22] Leadership scholars call this the beginning of the "trait" era. Researchers wondered about and studied what it was that some leaders had learned, been trained in, and cultivated in themselves that made them great.

Clinton continues:

---

[22] Clinton, *Short History of Leadership Theory*, 20.

It was characteristics of leaders and not the leaders themselves which were in focus. Additionally, the research was clearer. It had been assumed that Great Men just happened as a result of heredity and could be studied and admired but not replicated. But trait theorists were suggesting that perhaps leaders indeed could be made—that is, if common traits existed then perhaps some of them could be developed by training.[23]

Both Great Man Theory and Trait Theory focused on the singular leader rather than *leadership* itself. This is an important distinction to recognize. Edwin Hollander, an acclaimed social psychologist specializing in organizational dynamics, observes, "Leadership is not confined to a single person in a group but depends upon other members as well. Yet the terms *leadership* and *leader* are still used as if they were the same. For instance, the statement 'We need new leadership' usually means that another leader, with different characteristics, is needed."[24] His point is worth considering. When a leadership failure occurs, we rarely seek a new leadership system. We usually seek a new leader.

Hollander's perspective is in sync with the leadership theory era that rose in the late 1940s. Experts began to consider the group or organizational factors related to the leaders. "Group Theory" came to the fore, and the dynamics of interpersonal relationships and differing personality makeups were taken into account when considering good leadership. This discipline explores the role of leaders in influencing group behavior, facilitating effective communication, managing conflicts, and promoting cohesion. Leaders in this context often focus on creating an environment that fosters collaboration, motivation, and teamwork. Organizational life and management became the prevailing issue from this point forward.

---

[23] Ibid., 21.

[24] Edwin Paul Hollander, *Leadership Dynamics: A Practical Guide to Effective Relationships* (New York, NY: The Free Press, 1978), 2–3.

It is clear that our present-day concepts of leadership have arrived much more from modernity's cultural and institutional evolution than from universally defined terms. Although the study of leadership reaches back to antiquity—most notably in Chinese classics and in Plato, Caesar, Machiavelli, and Plutarch—most scholars point to a series of recent phases that have delivered our modern notions of leadership. Keep in mind that we further get into the weeds when we embrace leadership concepts that are from the kingdoms and powers of the world's systems rather than the kingdom of heaven, where God's power is "made perfect in weakness" (2 Corinthians 12:9).

Scholars who have sought to understand what we perceive today as "leadership" strongly agree it has come about from a stew of ideologies such as Great Man Theory and Trait Theory, along with a viewpoint positioned in Group Theory. Day to day, it mostly operates from the management dynamics founded upon what is commonly called "Taylorism."

## The Impact of Taylorism

Frederick Winslow Taylor was an engineer for the famed manufacturer, Bethlehem Steel. In 1911, he published *The Principles of Scientific Management,* which was born from the methods he had developed and implemented at that company. His theories arose from his experiments to achieve maximum efficiency, resulting in a system of clearly defined rules of operation. Taylor's principles continue to be implemented widely in contemporary industry and throngs of management sectors.

To be fair, Taylor's stated motive was to not only secure the maximum profit for the employer but also to seek the maximum pay for employees—believing a rising tide raises all boats.[25]

---

[25] Taylor wrote on the first page of his book: "In the same way maximum prosperity for each employee means not only higher wages than are usually received by men of his class, but, of more importance still, it also means the development of each man to his state of maximum efficiency, so that he may be able to do, generally speaking, the highest grade of work for which his natural abilities fit him." Frederick Winslow Taylor, *The Principles of Scientific Management* (Garden City, NY: Dover Publications, 1998), 1.

The reason Taylor's methods received the designation "scientific management" was because he used a diagnostic research approach to develop superior leadership systems. His aim was efficiency. Using stopwatches and charts, he recorded every action and movement of a worker doing a specific task. His ledger books were filled with his findings, and he used them to create rules of management and procedures for scale and profit. His experiments created performance thresholds; when a worker proved himself to be more efficient, they paid him a higher wage. Yet, each worker was under strict supervision and stern bosses. The "management era" had been born.

> The work of every man is fully planned out by the management at least one day in advance, and each man receives in most cases complete written instructions, describing in detail the task which he is to accomplish, as well as the means to be used in doing the work. This task specifies not only what is to be done but how it is to be done and the exact time allowed for doing it.[26]

Taylor established a clear division between labor and management, based on conclusions he had reached. At the core of his ideology was a firm belief that 99 percent of people could not be trusted to work hard enough apart from external rules; and that the typical employee tended to be lazy, seeking the easiest path. "For every individual ... who is overworked, there are a hundred who intentionally underwork—greatly underwork—every day of their lives."[27]

Along with his unabashed viewpoint that the typical employee was lazy, Taylor believed most frontline workers were incompetent to understand scientific methods. Therefore, it was incumbent upon management to provide the guidance and external pressure to get the most production possible from each worker.

---

[26] Ibid., 17.

[27] Ibid., 5.

Taylor was successful in reaching many of his goals, and credit is due to him for many positive outcomes for industry—including an increase in profits for owners and wages for workers. The problem for the church is when we import these ways and means into the kingdom endeavors of churches.

The entire theory of scientific management is based on the skewed belief that people are lazy, motivated by money, and don't have the mental capacity to make the best use of their time on the job. This doesn't consider an individual's character and calling—key components for serving in the kingdom of God. Taylorism brought with it a strict dichotomy between workers and management: "It is also clear that in most cases one type of man is needed to plan ahead and an entirely different type to execute the work."[28]

The impact of Taylor on our current leadership and management ideology is incalculable. I sincerely believe most leaders in the church who work from his paradigm merely do so because "managing people" is the only leadership style they have ever seen. Reflecting on the impact of Taylor's theories, renowned consultant and author Jeffrey Nielson writes:

> Taylor believed that leadership must be imposed from the top down in a command-and-control manner. The brains and intelligence of a company resided at the top, while the muscle for doing the actual work resided at the bottom. Today the belief that employees tend to be lazy and require external motivation is part of the unconscious fabric of leadership thought and practice. It creates a self-fulfilling prophecy, where seeing employees as lazy and unmotivated creates an organizational culture where the employees become lazy and unmotivated. When managers treat their employees as unmotivated "cost centers" who require constant supervision, employees become defensive and respond by doing the bare minimum to avoid mistakes or standing out. It doesn't take long for an employee who started

---

[28] Ibid., 16.

out with great enthusiasm to become dependent on the rank-base leader's management of all important decisions, until soon the employee loses all initiative. New hires in a rank-based organization come to work full of innovative ideas and energy only to retreat into a compliant "just doing what I'm told" mentality after repeatedly being put in their place by some threatened rank-based manager.[29]

Apart from outright narcissists, there is little doubt that very few church leaders actually believe their staff members are incompetent. So why do we embrace people management so strongly? The problem lies in the ways and means that have been passed along over decades. It is akin to the oft-told story of the young wife who cut off both ends of a ham before placing it in the oven. When her husband asked her why she did this, she told him that she had learned it from her mother, who had learned it from her own mother. She eventually discovered that her grandmother cut off both ends of the ham before putting it in the oven because her pan was too small for the whole ham.

So much of what we do in the kitchen of church leadership is because we saw our forebears do it that way. We believe people must be managed because ... well ... we've just always done it that way. In doing so, we fail to recognize that people end up being treated *as if* they are indeed incompetent, unmotivated, untrustworthy, and in need of upper-echelon managers to tell them how and when to do their jobs. It is a vicious soul-and-creativity-crushing cycle for both the one being managed and the one doing the managing. The waste of time and energy for both parties is lamentable.

Managing others in this fashion can have a hugely detrimental impact on the other person's sense of calling. It has become widely acceptable in church staff cultures for bosses and department heads to arbitrarily reassign staff members to stations or jobs they neither feel called to nor have a desire to occupy. There is no need to sugarcoat this.

---

[29] Jeffrey Nielson, *The Myth of Leadership: Creating Leaderless Organizations* (Palo Alto, CA: Davies-Black, 2004), 22–23.

No leader in the church has the right or God-given authority to do that. Such practices are in direct disobedience to Jesus' orders, which forbid lording over and dominating others. It is a "Gentile" way of operating.

## The Impact of Secular Leadership Theories on Church Leadership

The twentieth century sparked a virtual wildfire of leadership material in the corporate business and academic worlds. The church world, however, was producing very little in the way of leadership books and periodicals. But the roaring blaze of the church-growth movement needed fuel for the bonfire of bigger and better ministries, so churches relied on secular theories to build their approach.

As mentioned earlier, it has not been just large churches that have adopted secular methods. If you were to ask just about any pastor to share a list of ten *classic* books on different theological subjects, they would not struggle to come up with examples. The problem would be in whittling the list down to a mere ten. Names such as Calvin, Augustine, Wesley, Aquinas, and Chesterton would be on some lists. But if you were to ask the same pastor—who most likely has read a multitude of leadership books—to list ten *classic* Christian books on leadership, the names on that list would not go back very far.

Oswald Sander's 1967 book, *Spiritual Leadership*, is at or near the top in most surveys of the best Christian leadership texts of all times.[30] But it is hard to find more than a handful of Christian books with the word "leadership" in the title written prior to the 1960s. I spoke with the owner of one of the largest used Christian bookstores in the United States and asked him if he knew of any Christian books with the word "leadership" in the title prior to Sander's work. The guy is a walking bibliography on Christian books, but he could not come up with a single text. Perhaps the largest online retailer of used books, AbeBooks,

---

[30] J. Oswald Sanders, *Spiritual Leadership: Principles of Excellence For Every Believer* (Chicago, IL: Moody Press, 1967).

returned eleven thousand volumes when I entered the search query for "Christian leadership books," but only nine of them had the word "leadership" in the title and were published before Sander's work. I could find less than twenty such Christian books that were published in the 1970s.

The conclusion? If *leadership* as a scholarly topic in the broader world is an infant in diapers, then *Christian leadership* as a scholarly topic is an embryo. With such sparse content on Christian leadership, pastors turned to the business world to figure out how to lead bigger and better. Church-growth theory had *worked*—but now that they had built huge churches, pastors began to wonder how they would operate them. Willow Creek Community Church, in the suburban outskirts of Chicago, led the way. Its founding pastor, Bill Hybels, had developed the prototypical church that looked to be hitting on all cylinders of church-growth theory and was the leading innovator in the field. Willow Creek was the church thousands of church planters and pastors sought to imitate. No less than the Harvard Business School developed a case study on the ways and means of Willow Creek Community Church.

At its apex, Willow Creek was arguably the most prominent shaper of leadership thinking among evangelical churches, both large and small. The late founder of Leadership Network, Bob Buford, said, "Willow Creek is the most influential Protestant church in the world—one might even say the most influential church in the world save for the Vatican."[31] Their Global Leadership Summit soon became an annual pilgrimage for pastors and church leaders across North America. Those who could not make the trek to Chicago could join via satellite at host locations throughout the world to learn from a buffet of voices and methods mixed in with the pursuit of "redemptive potential"—Hybels's go-to phrase.

At its height, the summit had over six hundred satellite locations in the US, with around 260,000 leaders and fifteen thousand churches

---

[31] Jeff Chu, "How Willow Creek is Leading Evangelicals by Learning From the Business World," *Fast Company*, December 6, 2010, https://www.fastcompany.com/1702221/how-willow-creek-leading-evangelicals-learning-business-world.

taking part. Speakers included corporate and political titans and authors such as General Electric's Jack Welch, CEO of Hewlett-Packard Carly Fiorina, President Bill Clinton, Secretary of State Colin Powell, Prime Minister Tony Blair, Malcolm Gladwell, Jim Collins, and others. Summarizing the intent of the GLS, Hybels said, "We try to find people with the most thoughtful ideas about leadership, and we ask them to take their expertise and learning and spread it out over our audience." He sold the events as "the blend of high-impact, God-honoring messages with savvy, street-smart, don't-spiritualize-everything lessons from business."[32]

But it would all come crashing down. As the green curtain was pulled away, the behind-the-scenes tactics of Willow Creek's own leadership system were revealed. The distillation of leadership expertise they endorsed had generated a culture of bullying, pulling of rank, intimidation, selfish ambition, sexual abuse, and domineering tactics that were found to be the norm at the top levels of Willow Creek.[33]

Bill Hybels had built a virtual empire on "leadership competency." Now, Willow Creek, his legacy, was bankrupt of that very commodity. The days and months following his forced 2018 resignation saw mass resignations of staff members, turnover of the elder board, public apologies, and a mass exodus of church members. The most influential church of its time—the leading voice of leadership architecture for the evangelical church world—became a case study on how *not* to lead as Jesus would have us do so. As of this writing (2024), Hybels has not been heard from in the media or church platforms since his forced resignation for leadership abuse.

Not only did Willow Creek experience a failure of leadership, but its leadership also failed to produce what all churches are commanded to make: disciples of Christ. In 2007, Willow Creek Church's own Reveal

---

[32] Ibid.

[33] Laurie Goodstein, "How the Willow Creek Scandal Has Stunned the Evangelical World," *The New York Times*, August 10, 2018, https://www.nytimes.com/2018/08/09/us/evangelicals-willow-creek-scandal.html.

study, which included surveys of thirty thousand church members, concluded that "increasing levels of participation in these sets of activities [church programs] does NOT predict whether someone's becoming more of a disciple of Christ. It does NOT predict whether they love God more or they love people more."[34] All the "successful" church growth programs and leadership structures had collapsed under their own weight.

I take no joy in writing the above. But failing to acknowledge the damage caused by the paradigmatic leadership viewpoints coming from Willow Creek and spread among untold thousands of church leaders is tantamount to ignoring not just an elephant but a wooly mammoth in the room of the church.

## GOING BACK TO THE CODEBOOK

Leadership theories of the past have created the scenery and pathways for our own journeys. The combination of those theories—along with books, articles, conferences, and influencers—has shaped us to greater or lesser degrees. We have looked to great men and women and sought to be made in their image. We have attempted to imitate the habits, behavior, and traits of successful and admired leaders.

The industrial leadership approach to church leadership caused us to abandon the understanding of the church as a body and to turn to a view of the church as a machine. Our language and titles changed as we veered away from the code of the New Testament and Jesus. It became normal to hear terms and titles such as "strategic initiative," "ROI" (return on investment), "scale," "engineering," "management," "executive," and "superior" replace biblical language such as "steward," "disciple," "co-laborer," "servant," "minister," "elder," "brothers and sisters." Non-competes, NDAs, and HR became leverage points that

---

[34] Chuck Warnock, "Willow Creek Study Says Church Programs Don't Work," ChuckWarnock. com, October 24, 2007, https://chuckwarnockblog.wordpress.com/2007/10/24/willow-creek-study-says-church-programs-dont-make-better-disciples/.

displaced loving your brother or sister, blessing those you believed were your enemy, and letting your "yes be yes" and your "no be no" (Matthew 5:37). In doing so, we quenched the Spirit of familial compassion, shoved aside the priority of love above all things, ignored the fruit of the Spirit as a nonnegotiable leadership ethic, and failed to experience the distributed intelligence of the Head throughout the body.

Hopefully, this chapter has helped reveal the roots of our prevailing leadership and management paradigms. As we move forward, may we keep this brief history lesson in mind, paying careful attention as wise master builders when we choose our materials and methods.

## For Teams to Process

- How have the traditional leadership and management theories of the past century influenced the way we lead and manage in our church?
- In what ways have we adopted a business-oriented approach to leading and managing in our church?
- How have these traditional theories affected the way we view and treat our staff and church members?
- In what ways have we emphasized measurable outcomes and efficiency over holistic care for our staff and church members?
- How can we balance the principles of effective leadership and management with the teachings of Jesus and the values of the church?

# 3

# A DIFFERENT ATLAS

## Everything Rises and Falls on Headship

*Go stand at the crossroads and look around. Ask for directions to the old road, The tried-and-true road. Then take it. Discover the right route for your souls.*

JEREMIAH 6:16 MSG

*The great Christian revolutions came not by the discovery of something that was not known before. They happen when someone takes radically something that was always there.*

H. RICHARD NIEBUHR

After looking at the X-rays, my chiropractor asked if I had played football. Raising an eyebrow, I glanced at her and mumbled, "I'm from Texas." She chuckled, "Say no more." When a boy grows up in the Lone Star State, odds are he slipped into a set of shoulder pads and snapped on a chinstrap at some point or another. My Aussie friends and I constantly debate which game is rougher: rugby or American football. They argue, "You guys wear all that armor, but we are out there with what we were born with!" We might have had more protective gear, but back in my day, coaches taught us to lead with our heads when tackling. So that's what we did. We used our helmets as a weapon and drove into the ball carrier. Over and over.

Following thousands of spinal cord and brain injuries suffered by players, not only is the "lead with your head" technique not taught in football today, but it is also outlawed at every level. Players are now immediately ejected from a game if they do it. My chiropractor showed me the evidence of a chipped vertebra, along with other misaligned vertebrae below. I wasn't aware of when it had happened, but according to her, the damage most likely had been on the gridiron in my younger days and was finally demanding to be dealt with. So, over the next several months, I had a standing weekly appointment for treatment and realignment.

Just when I thought my interactions with chiropractors were mostly in the past, I received a response to one of my Facebook posts from a chiropractor from St. Louis. Frankly, I don't even remember exactly what I posted, but it was something about the body of Christ and leadership dysfunction. Dr. Eddie Weller commented that what I was describing was like *subluxation*—a condition in which the top two vertebrae in the spine misalign, causing the spine to be both neurologically and structurally compromised. The top vertebra is called the *atlas* (C-1) vertebra. Imagine that. *Atlas*. It relates to the *axis* (C-2) vertebra, which functions to protect the brainstem.

Considering the metaphor of Atlas I have already referred to—of leaders holding all the weight on their shoulders—I found the idea of a *different* atlas intriguing. So I went down a rabbit hole researching the C-1 vertebra.

## ATLAS MISALIGNMENT CAUSES PROBLEMS

A few chiropractors only practice what is known as "upper-cervical" care. They focus on the atlas and axis vertebrae and are not concerned so much with the others below that point. They don't do a lot of snapping, popping, or cracking on the rest of the back. Their philosophy is that if you get the C1 and C2 in order, everything below will eventually align and straighten out. When misaligned, this is the only location in the nervous system that affects the entire body and causes a neurological imbalance.

Our body's nervous system enables every element to operate—organs, cells, tissue, and limbs. It affects us emotionally, physically, and psychologically. When the spinal cord holding that system is in subluxation, our body doesn't function normally, much less optimally. Many patients receiving upper-cervical care have testified to healing or marked improvement of a myriad of maladies, including high blood pressure, digestive issues, allergies, fibromyalgia, white cell blood count, and others.

In his book *It Just Makes Sense*, Dr. Weller writes,

> There is that "extra-something" inside each and every one of us that gives life. This inborn "innate" intelligence knows what to do and how to do it. The intelligence (that came from our creator) travels in and through your nerve system, which is commonly referred to as the neurological system. (Neuro-logic or intelligence within the nerve). The neurologic communication between the brain and the body through the brainstem is imperative for allowing the body the best ability to function at its optimum. We believe that the body does not need any assistance, just no interference to its functioning.[1]

Upper-cervical care works to pinpoint misalignments and adjust the subluxation to restore proper function of the body's nervous system—where the intelligence of the head is distributed to the whole body. This aspect of God's design of the human body gives us a picture of the body of Christ—the church. And it also gives us clues as to why—despite decades of focus on more and *better* leadership—we have so much dysfunction, pain, and immobility in the church. Why do so many church and ministry leaders fall, under charges of bullying and misuse

---

[1] Eddie Weller, *It Just Makes Sense: Your Guide to Upper Cervical Chiropractic Care* (Chatham, NJ: Bowker, 2019), xi.

of power? Why can't we move past this continual cycle of leadership failure? Why is the church paralyzed in this area?

Perhaps the way God created the body to function physiologically reflects how we are to function spiritually as the body of Christ. Is it possible that the body of Christ continues to experience poor health, at least partially, because our prevailing leadership structures are misaligned with the Head—Jesus? And are we creating further misalignment by trying to be mini-Atlases instead of maintaining a faithful relationship with Jesus, the true Atlas (the true Head)?

In *A Failure of Nerve*, leadership consultant and rabbi Edwin Friedman writes,

> For in any age, concepts of leadership must square with the latest understanding of the relationship between brain and body. Recent findings about the brain-body connection have the potential to revolutionize our concept of hierarchy. For they suggest that to a large extent we have a liquid nervous system. The brain turns out to function like a gland. It is the largest organ of secretion, communicating simultaneously with various parts of the body, both near and far, through the reciprocal transmission of substances known as neurotransmitters. In other words, the head is *present* in the body![2]

This is God's design for the human body, but a state of subluxation circumvents the presence of the head in the body. The messages of the head cannot reach the body because the body's relationship with the head is disrupted. Not only are pain and malady a constant, but movement is also limited or halted. The body cannot live and move as intended.

Pain and disease are symptoms and messages from the body that there is a deeper problem. They're a built-in warning system—red

---

[2]  Edwin Friedman, *A Failure of Nerve: Leadership in the Age of the Quick Fix*, eds. Margaret M. Treadwell and Edward W. Beal (New York, NY: Seabury, 2007), 16–17.

lights flashing, sirens blaring—danger, danger! But upper-cervical care chiropractors don't throw more and better medicine at symptoms; they focus on the *system*. Their goal is not pain management. They seek to identify the place of misalignment and adjust at that spot, restoring the body to proper neurological form and function.

In church leadership, our analysis has tended to focus on the symptoms. We seem willing to look at any area other than the system itself. We crack, snap, pop, and adjust everywhere in leadership other than zeroing in on the most vital point of connection between the Head and the body. This is all futile if we don't get to the root of the issue.

## ATLAS MISALIGNMENT IN THE CHURCH

I know you didn't pick up this book to learn about the spine or to plumb the depths of chiropractic practice. And I am not proposing that Paul was thinking about twenty-first-century chiropractic treatment when he used the analogy of the body of Christ. However, given his repeated use of this metaphor and the language he employs to describe the body of Christ's relationship to Jesus as Head, it warrants a closer look.

The fourth chapter of Ephesians has received a lot of attention in recent years. It is here we find what has been termed *APEST*. Verse 12 speaks of the grace gifts (*charisms*) Jesus resources the body of Christ with—apostle, prophet, evangelist, shepherd, and teacher. I will not take time to dive deeply into that subject, as far better scholars than I have already done so extensively.[3] But take note that we have done a huge disservice to the church over the years when we have wrongly viewed this as a *leadership* text. Ephesians is written to the church as a whole. It is a text about the body of Christ, its proper alignment to

---

[3] For example, see Alan Hirsch, *5Q: Reactivating the Original Intelligence and Capacity of the Body of Christ* (Atlanta, GA: 100 Movements, 2017); Neil Cole, *Primal Fire: Reigniting the Church with the Five Gifts of Jesus* (Carol Stream, IL: Tyndale House, 2014).

the headship of Jesus, and how the gifts given by the Lord Jesus should function in the body.

In their book *The Permanent Revolution*, Alan Hirsch and Tim Catchim say,

> Even when these verses are taken seriously by various churches and denominations … by far the most common way that APEST has been read is to identify it as the leadership of the church. As the idea states it, Jesus has equipped *some* in the body in order to train all the *others* to do ministry. At first glance, this seems to make a lot of sense: the church staff equips the members to do ministry. Unfortunately, this interpretation of the text is a by-product of the institutional ways we organize ourselves and fails to recognize the movemental nature of ecclesia in the New Testament.[4]

Ephesians chapter four is for and about the body of Christ and the gifts Jesus has given to each member for the sake of the whole as it pursues faithful mission.

> There is one body and one Spirit, just as you were called to one hope when you were called; one Lord, one faith, one baptism; one God and Father of all, who is over all and through all and in all.

> But to each one of us grace has been given as Christ apportioned it. This is why it says:

> "When he ascended on high,
>     he took many captives
>     and gave gifts to his people."
>     EPHESIANS 4:4–8 NIV

Paul says that the five key gifts (APEST) help the body reach unity, maturity, and the fullness of Christ.

---

[4] Alan Hirsch and Tim Catchim, *The Permanent Revolution: Apostolic Imagination and Practice for the 21st Century Church* (San Francisco, CA: Jossey-Bass, 2012), 21.

> Until we all reach unity in the faith and in the knowledge of the Son of God and become mature, attaining to the whole measure of the fullness of Christ. Then we will no longer be infants, tossed back and forth by the waves, and blown here and there by every wind of teaching and by the cunning and craftiness of people in their deceitful scheming.
>
> EPHESIANS 4:13–14 NIV

When the body of Christ is aligned with the headship of Jesus and uses all its gifts, it leads to unity of purpose. It helps move the church beyond acting like children and brings stability, eliminating flightiness and susceptibility to the deceitfulness of charlatans. Tragically, we witness these negative aspects all too frequently in the church today. The key to fullness in Christ has everything to do with Head/body alignment.

> But speaking the truth in love, we are to grow up in all *aspects* into Him who is the head, *that is*, Christ, from whom the whole body, being fitted and held together by what every joint supplies, according to the proper working of each individual part, causes the growth of the body for the building up of itself in love.
>
> EPHESIANS 4:15–16 NASB

Notice the connection Paul makes between Jesus as Head and his body—the church. He says we are joined to the Head in correlation to the key joints. In the human body, the joints that connect the body to the head begin with the atlas vertebra. Try as we might for more and better "leadership"—being better Atlases—there is no substitute for the body of Christ being in proper systemic alignment with our true Atlas, allowing the body to function properly.

In the same way that throwing drugs at pain does not deal with the root issue, so trying to numb our leadership symptoms with better management and leadership techniques is not the answer. Though we have believed that churches rise and fall on their leader, in reality, everything rises or falls on headship, and the whole body's alignment with that Head. Each individual part (member) can only work properly together if the whole body is properly aligned to its Head: Jesus. Just as a human body can have healthy limbs yet be in a state of paralysis if the spinal system is injured or out of whack, so a church can remain dysfunctional, diseased, or immobilized if the overriding leadership system circumvents proper alignment with the true Head. Everything rises or falls on the headship of Jesus.

Misalignment happens when we begin to look more like the world than Christ. In Romans 12, Paul develops the metaphor of the church as the body of Christ. But before he talks about how the body of Christ is to function, he encourages his hearers to not be conformed to this world.

> Therefore, I urge you, brothers and sisters, in view of God's mercy, to offer your bodies as a living sacrifice, holy and pleasing to God—this is your true and proper worship. Do not conform to the pattern of this world, but be transformed by the renewing of your mind. Then you will be able to test and approve what God's will is—his good, pleasing and perfect will.
>
> ROMANS 12:1–2 NIV

This passage is most often used as a stand-alone quote to remind us not to be worldly. We tend to think of "worldliness" as participating in vices such as sexual immorality, drunkenness, carousing, and the like. Back in the day, fundamentalist Christians would say, "Don't smoke, drink, or chew. And don't run around with those that do."

But Paul never limited the idea of worldliness to acts such as carousing and sexual impropriety. He was speaking of anything and everything that comes from the fallen cultural ways of the kingdoms of the world. A fair interpretation could be, "Don't think like the common person, who has no working relationship with Jesus, functions according to the prevailing systems of the world, and is not seeking the agenda of the kingdom of heaven."

For Christians, the subtle danger happens when we *conform*—the word Paul uses here. It puzzles us when seemingly good leaders have a moral failure or a scandalous fall from grace. We wonder why so many pastors and leaders who start out so well—so Jesus-like—in the beginning, eventually become something different. But this is seldom a sudden change. It happens over time.

Revelations from recent evangelical leadership scandals, where some of the most famous and influential pastors of our time went down in flames, have shed light on how each of them lorded over and dominated those around them for years. Staff members and church members have come forward with consistent and repeated examples of bullying, arrogance, and systemic abuse from the pastors who were eventually removed. The way they talked to others and carried themselves was a giveaway that they were guilty of "leadership intoxication." If you've ever witnessed a group of drunk people, they just keep drinking until the hootch is gone or they pass out. It goes that far because the entire group is drinking, and there's no sober person around to put an end to it.

## LEADERSHIP INTOXICATION
## MAKES THE BODY STUMBLE

Just before going into a lengthy discourse on the differing functions of members (parts) of the body of Christ in Romans 12, Paul again warns us to stay sober and not conform to the patterns of this world.

> For by the grace given to me I say to everyone among you: Do not think of yourself more highly than you ought, but rather think of yourself with sober judgment, in accordance with the faith God has distributed to each of you. For just as each of us has one body with many members, and these members do not all have the same function, so in Christ we, though many, form one body, and each member belongs to all the others. We have different gifts, according to the grace given to each of us. [Use your gift] in accordance with your faith.
>
> ROMANS 12:3–6 NIV

Paul warns against the dark side of being gifted—thinking of oneself more highly than one should. In fact, he tells us not to be drunk on the arrogance of giftedness.

The early church was charismatic. Not charismatic as in the hyped-up expressions we sometimes see today, but in terms of the biblical, literal Greek word *charisma*, which speaks of the spiritual gifts administrated by the Holy Spirit. Sadly, we have elevated the *charisma* of the Spirit above the fruit of the Spirit.

Leadership can easily turn into a power trip. People have a propensity to become intoxicated on positional power. If you have ever lived in a neighborhood with a Home Owners Association (HOA), you know this all too well!

When a person becomes drunk with power in the church, they usurp Jesus' rightful position as Head of the body of Christ, and the members become effectively paralyzed. This misalignment with the Head cuts off the members from functioning in their gifts and callings. They become largely dormant apart from being consumers of religious goods and services.

Paul reminds his hearers to stay sober in their thinking in relationship to their particular function. In essence, he says, "You are only a body part, just like everyone else in the body. So get over yourself."

But let's not miss how Paul starts off this strong warning. He says, "For by the grace given to me, I say ..." He includes himself in the alert he is about to give. He starts by identifying himself as one who owes everything—his gifting and function—to grace. Over the next few sentences, Paul continues to include himself in the warning with multiple uses of the words "we" and "us." Regardless of the incredible giftings and stature he has, he is pointing out that he is merely another body part, just like everyone else.

> For just as each of us has one body with many members, and these members do not all have the same function, so in Christ *we*, though many, form one body, and each member belongs to *all* the others.
>
> ROMANS 12: 4–5 NIV (EMPHASES MINE)

Here we see the unique nature of community in Christ. The characteristics of connection include diverse parts and functions, yet an overarching unity not only of purpose but of the life as a whole. "The unity is due to the principle of life which animates the entire body—in the case of the church, to Christ as the head."[5] In worldly communities, differences often bring dissension. Competitiveness, jealousy, and the like enter in. The beauty of the body of Christ is that, when functioning healthily, diversity doesn't cause division. Our differences are our strengths. Each member supplies what the others lack, and no members set themselves above others. Mutual respect, reliance, and accountability reside in the human body and must do the same in the body of Christ for healthy functionality.

If you are American and old enough to have watched *The Andy Griffith Show*, you probably remember Barney Fife, the bumbling but good-hearted deputy. In one episode, Otis, the town drunk, spikes the water cooler at the sheriff's office with moonshine. As Barney drinks from the "water," he slowly but surely goes from tipsy to full-blown drunk—or "gassed" as Andy says.[6]

In the church, rather than aligning to the headship of Christ, gifted people sip from the bottle of leadership and end up intoxicated by power. They slowly but surely drift into the depths of the ways of the present age. They eventually bend to—or *conform*—to the ways of the fallen world and its systems. The inebriation of pride, arrogance, and popularity moves into the bloodstream and overrides the influence of God's grace that once prevailed in hearts and minds. Just as an alcoholic knows another alcoholic when they see one, so a leaderoholic knows another leaderoholic when they see one.

When I started out as a church planter, I had every intention of developing a team. My heart was to see everyone flourish and for each

---

[5] George Arthur Buttrick, *The Interpreter's Bible: The Holy Scriptures in the King James and Revised Standard Versions with General Articles and Introduction, Exegesis, Exposition for Each Book of the Bible, Vol. IX* (Nashville, TN: Abingdon Press, 1954), 584.

[6] The Andy Griffith Show, season 3, episode 15, "Barney and the Governor," first aired January 7, 1963, https://www.imdb.com/title/tt0512448/.

member of our staff to have a voice and grow into their full potential. Along the way, our quick growth and "success" caused me to conform to the world's ways of leading. I became the boss. And it came at a cost. I made some unwise unilateral decisions that damaged relationships and resulted in the loss of a few incredibly gifted members of our team. It hurt them, my wife, me, and the church. I got drunk on leadership. I was not a mean drunk; but I was a drunk boss—what is commonly known as a benevolent dictator.

If I had realized there was something in the leadership water I was guzzling and stayed "sober," there is no doubt in my mind we would have been a much healthier church in the long run. But my modus operandi was to unilaterally call the shots and make wide-ranging decisions on my own.

Maybe we should install a field sobriety test in our churches for those in leadership positions. When a police officer suspects a person is publicly intoxicated or is operating a motor vehicle under the influence of alcohol, speech patterns and body language usually tip them off. The way a person talks and walks gives off clues as to sobriety or intoxication. It is the same when people are no longer aligned with Christ and instead are drunk on power. How they speak to others can often be a giveaway regarding abusive tendencies. Some common phrases or speech patterns that dominating leaders may use on subordinates include:

- "You need to listen to me because I've been called to lead this church."
- "You don't have the experience or knowledge to make that decision."
- "Are you questioning me?"
- "I don't have time to explain my reasoning. Just do as I say."
- "I'm the one in charge here, so you need to follow my lead."

Such phrases and speech patterns are used to assert dominance and control over others and often discourage independent thought or decision-making. They can create an unhealthy dynamic in a church, as they undermine the authority of Jesus as the Head of the body and foster unhealthy power dynamics within the church body.

## JESUS FILLS THE BODY WITH HIMSELF

In Paul's opening salutation to the Ephesians, he plants a stake in the ground that was to remain a splinter in their mind:

> *I pray that* the eyes of your heart may be enlightened, so that you will know what is the hope of His calling, what are the riches of the glory of His inheritance in the saints, and what is the boundless greatness of His power toward us who believe. *These are* in accordance with the working of the strength of His might which He brought about in Christ, when He raised Him from the dead and seated Him at His right hand in the heavenly *places*, far above all rule and authority and power and dominion, and every name that is named, not only in this age but also in the one to come. And He put all things in subjection under His feet, and made Him head over all things to the church, which is His body, the fullness of Him who fills all in all.
>
> EPHESIANS 1:18–23 NASB

Jesus is the Head of his body—the church. And *all* rulership, power, authority, and dominion are his and his alone. All earthly and satanic power forms, iterations, and delivery systems that cloak themselves as wisdom, strategy, and envisioning are foreign to his ways.

Jesus, as Head of the body, fills the body with *himself.* The Head is in the whole body. He distills into it his love, joy, peace, wisdom, counsel, and power for the express purpose of the church reflecting his glory into the world. The body of Christ should manifest the fullness—the totality of expression—of Jesus on the earth. The inner connection of the body to itself and, most importantly, in proper order to Jesus, is crucial.

If we wonder why Paul's metaphor is so vivid, just consider where he most likely got it from. Originally known as Saul, Paul was a highly educated religious leader who was a fierce persecutor of the fledgling church. During one of his tyrannical campaigns to eliminate the upstart band of disciples, he was blinded by a heavenly flash of light, and he heard an audible voice asking, "Saul, Saul, why are you persecuting me?" (Acts 9:4). When he asked who it was that was speaking, Jesus identified himself: "I am Jesus, whom you are persecuting" (v. 5). The message was clear: mess with the church and you are messing with Jesus (his body).

In Saul's (Paul's) thinking, he was pursuing a cult that opposed the Lord, but he came to realize that he had been persecuting the Lord himself, who was *present* in every part of the church—the body of Christ. And Jesus dealt with him in the most astonishing manner. When a person goes through something like that, it sticks with them. From that day forward, when Paul thought of the church, he saw Jesus, the body of Christ.

Any dealings we have with the church today are an encounter with Jesus. This goes for leadership as well. If you are a pastor or a leader of any type of ministry, the people in your sphere of responsibility must be considered as if they are Jesus himself. For good or bad, the way we treat the secretary, the youth pastor, the janitor—everyone—is the way we are treating Jesus. Our attitude toward *all* members is our attitude toward Jesus. If we are a bully or a jerk to an associate pastor in the afternoon, we just pushed Jesus around. On the other hand, if we honor and bless a fellow staff member, we just blessed Jesus.

## REALIGNING TO THE HEADSHIP OF JESUS AS SERVANTS

In the passage we looked at several times earlier, where Jesus commands his disciples that "it will not be so among you" (Matthew 20:25–28), he says it is the Gentiles who practice lording over and dominating one another. The term "Gentile" is a metaphor for the ways of the fallen world: its systems and mode of operating. Jesus commands his followers to identify and function as *servants,* not as *leaders*—especially not the way the world's leaders operate.

Keep in mind, Jesus is the Head of the body of Christ; when we ignore his words, we misalign with our Head and become dysfunctional, immobilized, and diseased. We cease to follow him—his ways and means. Despite our preference for identifying as leaders, Scripture patently rejects such thinking. Jesus and the other New Testament writers consistently referred to Christ as a *servant,* not as a leader: "I am among you as the one who serves" (Luke 22:27).

Notice Jesus didn't say, "I am *over* you as the one who *leads.*" He said, "I am *among* you as the one who serves" (emphasis mine). What a simple yet profound statement! This is servant language. Was Jesus a leader? Without question, he was the best ever! But his *identity* was as a servant. His leadership was the fruit and outcome of his posture and self-identification as a servant. It was the way he thought. The key to Jesus' way of thinking is the Greek term *kenosis*: to empty. This is the very thing Paul implores us to do in the following passage:

> Do nothing out of selfish ambition or vain conceit. Rather, in humility value others above yourselves, not looking to your own interests but each of you to the interests of the others.
>
> In your relationships with one another, have the same mindset as Christ Jesus:

> > Who, being in very nature God,
> > did not consider equality with God
> > something to be used to his own advantage;
> > rather, he made himself nothing
> > by taking the very nature of a servant,
> > being made in human likeness.
> >
> > PHILIPPIANS 2:3–7 NIV

Commenting on this passage, author and leadership professor Bryan Sims writes,

At the heart of these verses, Paul is asking followers of Jesus to *empty themselves*. This is what it means to embody kenosis; and it flies in the face of our current solo-heroic paradigm of leadership, because when we truly embrace kenosis, we adopt the posture of a *servant*, not a *hero*. As leaders practice kenosis, we listen more than we talk. We operate in obedience to God and his will rather than pushing our own agenda. We become more concerned with "we" than "me." We look to the needs of others.[7]

Do we need leadership in the church? Absolutely. Do we need *better* leadership? That's an understatement. The error is that we have made leadership a *position* rather than a *product*—like fruit and vegetables. The person who cultivates fruit and vegetables does not call herself *a tomatoer* or *a cucumberer*; she is a gardener or a farmer, and the *outcome* of her work is *produce*—tomatoes and cucumbers. Leadership in the church must be seen in the same way—as an *outcome*. Good leadership in the church is the fruit of humble servants who have emptied themselves of selfish ambition. In the church, we are all servants, and the *outcome* of faithful servants is *leadership*.

Not only is it unnecessary to focus on leadership and *being* leaders, but it is also extremely problematic when we do so, especially because most people's concepts of leadership come from the paradigms of management and hierarchical systems and structures. The continued near-exclusive use of the terms "leader" and "leadership" comes at the expense of developing genuine Jesus-following servants.

I propose that servanthood is the Atlas vertebra in the body of Christ. It's the posture and pattern of Jesus and the identity and outlook he gave to his disciples. When we take on any other identity apart from that of a servant—including that of a *leader*—we are poised to enter a state of subluxation.

Paul prescribes the way to maintain the change: "Be transformed by the renewal of your mind" (Romans 12:2). Rather than being

---

[7] Sims, *Leading Together*, 7–8.

conformed to the world's thinking, we are to be transformed in our mindset and paradigm. The nutrients of renewal are the Living Water and the Bread of Life—Jesus and the Word of God. *The Interpreter's Bible* says, "The result of this transformation is the ability to prove, to discern in actual experience, what is the will of God. With a new sensitiveness of insight, we discover in our actual situation what God would have us do, and in the process, we learn more fully the nature of his purpose for us."[8]

I once heard someone say the problem with a *living* sacrifice is it keeps trying to crawl off the altar. When we let ourselves drift into conforming to the mindset of the fallen nature of humankind and worldly ways and agendas, we fail to offer ourselves as a living sacrifice. We stop giving ourselves, and what God has given us through grace, toward the will of God. Our hearts turn inward—toward seeking to place ourselves first rather than assuming the position of a servant. We use his grace gifts for our own devices and agendas. We build our own structures to prop up our own kingdoms and empires.

*The Interpreter's Bible* is helpful again:

> Anyone possessed of an inflated notion of his own importance is certain to see himself through a distorting medium of arrogance or complacency. He will misconceive his own function, and he will jeopardize his proper relationship to others. He will be wrong in his estimate of himself and of his proper contribution to the common life; and his mistake, because it is both insidious in character and inclusive in scope, will be particularly difficult to rectify.[9]

To think of oneself more *highly*, it is necessary to think of others more *lowly*. In our minds, we place ourselves above others. This is how hierarchy develops in the church. Theologically, we know better; but functionally we fall short. Our theological ducks sit in

---

[8] Buttrick, *The Interpreter's Bible*, Vol IX, 582.

[9] Ibid., 583.

a row on the back shelves of our mind. Our praxis overrides our theology because we believe we are better and more important than those around us.

When the inebriation of arrogance and pride sets in, entitlement goes to seed in the heart and mind. The arrogant leader believes they have the right to infringe upon the rights of others. They believe they have earned greater privileges than others. Individuals who yield to such temptations begin to treat those around them as lesser-than, lower-than.

When strongly gifted people fail to engage in a process of constant transformation of mind and heart through Christ, they are no longer recalibrating themselves to Christ and therefore no longer exude humility. Narcissism begins to manifest, along with its accompanying character traits. Professionals diagnose persons with Narcissistic Personality Disorder (a pervasive pattern of grandiosity [in fantasy or behavior], need for admiration, and lack of empathy) when they exhibit five or more of the following:

1. Has a grandiose sense of self-importance (e.g., exaggerates achievements and talents, expects to be recognized as superior without commensurate achievements)
2. Is preoccupied with fantasies of unlimited success, power, brilliance, beauty, or ideal love
3. Believes that he or she is "special" and unique and can only be understood by, or should associate with, other special or high-status people (or institutions)
4. Requires excessive admiration
5. Has a sense of entitlement, i.e., unreasonable expectations of especially favorable treatment or automatic compliance with his or her expectations
6. Is interpersonally exploitative, i.e., takes advantage of others to achieve his or her own ends
7. Lacks empathy: is unwilling to recognize or identify with the feelings and needs of others

8. Is often envious of others or believes that others are envious of him or her
9. Shows arrogant, haughty behaviors or attitudes."[10]

In the field of ministry, an inflated sense of self-importance tends to create a virtual firewall of entitlement. Galvanized by their God-given gifts—"God put me in this position; he ordained me and equipped me to be *the* leader in this church or ministry"—such persons view the value and giftings of others as less important and less deserving of honor and a listening ear. Postures such as this shut down the voices of others through sheer intimidation or outright pulling of rank. This puts the body out of joint with the Head. We become misaligned structurally and systemically because we fail to stay in line with our true Atlas—which is following Jesus' model as a servant.

The beauty of servantship is multifaceted. Not only does it center us in the mind of Christ, but it also cultivates the fruit of the Holy Spirit in our lives. However, good fruit doesn't grow in poor soil. The soil of our heart must be good. And we must be vigilant in examining the condition of our hearts. "Keep your heart with all vigilance, for from it flow the springs of life" (Proverbs 4:23).

Several years ago, my wife asked me to clear a plot of ground on our property for a garden. After a couple of weeks behind a teeth-chattering tiller, breaking ground in her chosen spot, I told her the garden was ready for planting. "Not quite yet," she replied. She wanted to have the soil analyzed first. When the results came in, it revealed a serious imbalance of particular nutrients. In short order, I was back behind the tiller for several days, blending a mix of minerals into the soil—to make it seed-ready. We ended up with an incredibly productive garden, which would not have happened without serious attention to the condition of the soil.

Worldly leadership methods and systems create poor heart

---

[10] *Diagnostic and Statistical Manual of Mental Disorders*, 4th ed. (Washington, DC: American Psychiatric Association, 2000), 714–15.

conditions for cultivating the fruit of the Spirit. It is a mismatch. It gives way to thorns and weeds of fleshly ways that choke out the gentleness, grace, goodness, kindness, patience, and meekness of the Spirit's work in the human psyche. For these reasons, identifying ourselves as servants is essential to our relationship with those around us. When I approach you from the perspective of a servant sent from the Lord to help you in your calling, rather than as a leader who feels you are here to learn from me or to serve my calling, everything changes. This requires relational intelligence and a degree of relational companionship that is not present in corporate cultures.

Many staff members have told me they've never had a personal conversation with their lead pastor; they have never shared a meal in that person's home and have never just hung out for hanging out's sake. Think about this in relation to serving. If I am here to serve you, I *must* have conversations with you. I will *want* to have conversations with you. I *need* to hear your heart, your desires, and your needs. How else can I serve you? If I approach you from the disposition of being your leader, the script is flipped. You are here to make sure my wants, needs, and agenda are tended to. And I justify my attitude by pointing to the mission or vision for the church—the greater purpose must be served. The *mission* becomes more important than the people who are on mission.

Servanthood, as a mindset and posture, constantly recalibrates our hearts and minds to our place in the body of Christ and to the value of others the Lord has joined us to. It keeps us in an "among others" posture rather than an "over others" position. At the heart of servanthood is a deep desire to help others. The prevailing mindset is, "How can I help the ones around me?" A servant places their own wants and needs at the back of the queue.

Robert Greenleaf, founder of the modern servant-leadership movement, once said,

> The servant-leader is servant first. It begins with the natural feeling
> that one wants to serve. Then conscious choice brings one to aspire

to lead. The best test is: do those served grow as persons; do they, while being served, become healthier, wiser, freer, more autonomous, more likely themselves to become servants?[11]

This is primary to being an equipper and discipler in any church or ministry. Are we producing servant-minded, servant-hearted disciples? Are we paying attention to their development at all?

While the lordship of Jesus revolves around our relationship with Jesus individually, the headship of Jesus has to do with our relationship with the body of Christ. Leadership systems that supplant Jesus as Chief Shepherd with a singular person or two at the top are disjointed from the true Head of the body. We may live under the lordship of Christ personally but be out of sorts with the headship of Christ in relationship with his body. Leadership culture in our churches is not a mere preference or choice; it has everything to do with whether Jesus is functionally the Head of our church.

## For Teams To Process

Look at the following statements that describe realignment to Christ's headship. As a team, evaluate how well you are expressing these values.

- We utilize resources and tools to discover all team members' gifts and key interests.
- We renew our systems and structures for a free flow of permission to share input of ideas and concerns regarding every area of the church.

---

[11] Robert K. Greenleaf, et al., *The Servant-Leader Within: A Transformative Path* (New York, NY: Paulist Press, 2003), 13.

- Every team member functions "among" one another. No individual is "over" another.
- We allow no quarter for selfish ambition or conceit.
- We count others as more significant than ourselves.
- No one gets perks or privileges that others are not allowed to receive.
- Each team member constantly and consciously looks out for the interests of their fellow team members.
- No one is allowed to use force, threats, intimidation, or inducement of fear upon another, regardless of status or experience.
- Leadership is defined as a fruit or outcome rather than a pursuit or position.
- We lay down our identity as leaders and view ourselves as mere servants of God, as expressed through our actions and interactions with one another.
- We nip narcissism in the bud by understanding what it is and what it looks like. We point out any hint of it when necessary.

# 4

# AUTHORITY, WARFARE, AND WEAKNESS

## Realigning Headship

*A leadership culture turns the church into an organization, governed by a set of management principles. It turns pastors into leaders whose primary aim is the success of the organization—based in some way on achievable metrics. The more ambitious the leader and the more narcissistic the leader, the less of a church the church becomes.*

SCOT MCKNIGHT AND LAURA BARRINGER

*Don't fool yourself. Don't think that you can be wise merely by being relevant. Be God's fool—that's the path to true wisdom. What the world calls smart, God calls stupid. It's written in Scripture, He exposes the hype of the hipsters. The Master sees through the smoke screens of the know-it-alls.*

1 CORINTHIANS 3:19 MSG

Growing up in the 1970s was great. We cruised to classic tunes before they were classics, watched Evel Knievel fly and crash live, dreamed of being one of the Dukes of Hazzard, and wore John-Travolta-inspired silk shirts and bell-bottom jeans. And something else: We played outdoors. The only video game we had was a contraption hooked up to our television that had a bouncing dot from one side of the screen to the other, with a line in the middle. It was called *Pong*. Basically, it was video tennis or ping-pong. And it was revolutionary! But after a while, you were ready to get up from sitting cross-legged on the shag carpet and do something else.

When there was no one else to play with, I could be found in our backyard, throwing a tennis ball against the brick wall at the back of our house. I had made up my own one-player baseball game. I caught fly balls that bounced off the roof and retrieved grounders, throwing them back against the wall so I could catch them before they hit the ground. And I was my own play-by-play announcer: "Ball bounced to shortstop. He throws to first. Out, number one!"

There was only one little window at the end of the house, and it opened to my parent's bathroom. I was always sure to steer clear of throwing anywhere near that little rectangle. But one Saturday afternoon as I was throwing the ball against the brick—as I had done literally thousands of times—*it* finally happened. I sent the ball careening against that frosted window. Tempered or double-paned glass in those days was rare, and the fragile glass offered no resistance to the fuzzy Spalding orb. *Smash!* The window went crashing into the bathroom.

It is important to understand that the far-from-fully-developed brain of an eleven-year-old boy can still do an enormous amount of quick calculating. It's an amazing little computer. In less than one second, I was already concocting a scheme to get out of this one (cue the *Mission Impossible* theme song):

- T minus 3: Assess—*Where's Dad? Maybe he's out working on his car or playing his guitar and didn't hear the ball against the wall, followed by the sound of breaking glass.*
- T minus 2: Strategize—*Maybe I could grab my BB gun, kill a bird, retrieve the tennis ball, leave the bird in the bathroom and the bird would be the culprit. Sorry, bird. We appreciate your sacrifice.*

- T minus 1: Initiate—*Yes. Excellent plan. Do it. Go, go, go!*
- T minus Zero: *Fail!*

Just as I was about to put the plan into action, I saw the top of my dad's head, slowly rising over the windowsill. Yep, the toilet was directly under that window. As Dad's face fully appeared, jet black hair sparkling with shards of frosted glass, his eyes met mine. And there it was. *The look.* The "How many times have I told you?" look. The "What were you thinking?" look. The "If I have to stop this car" look. The "Where's my belt?" look. Somewhere in the trees, a relieved mockingbird was chirping, "Not today, dude!"

You'd expect a grown man to be much larger than an eleven-year-old boy, but my dad was a big man, period. He was brawny, with Popeye-like forearms. He could have easily passed for an NFL middle linebacker. And he needed to shave twice a day to maintain a smooth face. Never once did a friend argue with me that his dad could whip my dad. My father could intimidate me if he needed to. The thing was … he didn't need to. He was naturally intimidating.

So, how did the bird and I live to see another day? Like a perfectly staged scene from a movie, just after he looked out to investigate the reason for the shattered window, my dad slowly sat back down, eyes locking with mine as he descended below the jagged remains of frosted glass. But he never said a word about the window. Not one word. The following Monday afternoon, Mr. Meisenheimer, who ran our town's only glass company and also happened to be my baseball coach, came out and measured the window for a replacement. As he pulled out his measuring tape, he raised an eyebrow, and with a sly grin said, "Lance, I thought I taught you to throw a little better than this." I never broke another window.

The authority my dad carried in my life went far beyond intimidation—a sign of true authority. His character, love, integrity, and knowing what needed to be said—and what didn't—epitomized his influence in my life. All that bore a lot more weight than brawn or disciplining every misstep. That is the difference between power and true authority. The more volume a person needs, the less clout they usually have. Just think of how loud (or not) you have to get for your dog to listen to you.

## THE COUNTERINTUITIVE NATURE
## OF SPIRITUAL AUTHORITY

In the Western world, we admire and idolize strong leaders who derive their authority from status, power, titles, or skills. But godly leadership derives its authority from servanthood, meekness, and sacrifice. Worldly leadership points only to itself and misaligns the body from the headship of Christ, but godly leadership's strength comes from its weakness and dependence on the headship of Christ. If we are to have godly leadership, we must have leaders who relinquish their power and authority and make room for God's power and authority. He must increase, and we must decrease.

In 2 Corinthians, none other than Paul the apostle had to defend his spiritual authority to the church at Corinth. I can't imagine such a titan would need to do such a thing, but he did. A faction of what Paul would sarcastically label "super-apostles" (2 Corinthians 11:5) had sown discord in the minds of the saints. And their attacks focused on Paul's posture and demeanor. A rising caucus was mounting against him, challenging his authority and accusing him of writing bold letters but being weak when he met them in person (2 Corinthians 10:10).

Think of the ways so many people today operate from *keyboard courage*—firing off curt comments and terse replies on social-media posts—writing things from a distance they would never have the guts to say to the person's face. Paul was being accused of this and found it necessary to explain his actions.

I am going to make an uncommon request at this point. Context is essential for us to understand the Scriptures, and because we are prone to reading stand-alone verses, we often lose the essence and intent of the text. It is not practical to include four full chapters of biblical text here, so, pause from this book for a moment, open your

Bible or Bible app, and read 2 Corinthians 10–13. After you do that, come right back.

Now that we have the picture of what Paul wants to convey, let's look closer. He is about to provide us with a succinct lesson on the nature of spiritual authority and its relationship to spiritual warfare (verse numbers are included here because we'll look at them in detail below):

> [1] By the humility and gentleness of Christ, I appeal to you—I, Paul, who am "timid" when face to face with you, but "bold" toward you when away! [2] I beg you that when I come I may not have to be as bold as I expect to be toward some people who think that we live by the standards of this world. [3] For though we live in the world, we do not wage war as the world does. [4] The weapons we fight with are not the weapons of the world. On the contrary, they have divine power to demolish strongholds. [5] We demolish arguments and every pretension that sets itself up against the knowledge of God, and we take captive every thought to make it obedient to Christ. [6] And we will be ready to punish every act of disobedience, once your obedience is complete.
>
> [7] You are judging by appearances. If anyone is confident that they belong to Christ, they should consider again that we belong to Christ just as much as they do. [8] So even if I boast somewhat freely about the authority the Lord gave us for building you up rather than tearing you down, I will not be ashamed of it.
>
> 2 CORINTHIANS 10:1–8 NIV

**"By the humility and gentleness of Christ, I appeal to you" (v. 1a)**
In this opening phrase, Paul confesses his meekness. He's guilty as charged. "Yes, I do come with a posture of meekness," he admits, but he points out that he operates "by the meekness and gentleness of Christ." He says the source of it is his formation in Jesus. His gentleness was a product of self-control, an essential fruit of the Spirit. The word

for "meekness" here is a Greek term, *prautēs,* which means "mildness of disposition." Interestingly, it is a feminine noun (the opposite of a macho persona). And this is very telling. The term is from the same root word Jesus used to describe himself: "I am meek and lowly in heart" (Matthew 11:29 KJV). The inward virtue of meekness produces the outward disposition of gentleness. In the commentary on 2 Corinthians 10:1–2, *The Interpreter's Bible* says,

> It was a humility and gentleness born of confidence in God and in his message. But this confidence could also make [Paul] bold in [Paul's accusers] sense of the word (v. 2), as those who accused him of a worldly spirit would discover. Some of his opponents had made this charge against him, which he now rebuts. He had not stooped to the methods of men of the world in his ministry, using cunning or deceit.[1]

**"I, Paul, who am 'timid' when face to face with you, but 'bold' toward you when away!" (v. 1b)**

Paul has equated his meekness with having a mild disposition, but here the word he uses is different. It is *tapeinos* and it has a completely different connotation. It is his accusers' word for "meek," which means, "from a base low degree or low estate." The word conveys the attitude, "You are a nothing." The juxtaposition of the two terms is fascinating. It is a brilliant use of linguistics on Paul's part to set up the lesson on spiritual authority he is about to embark on at length, taking up four chapters in the New Testament.

It is important we understand the point Paul is emphasizing by using two different words for "meek" here. He is quoting those who are opposing and debasing him. He is saying he has chosen a mild disposition, refusing to preen and posture, but his opponents have used this against him, interpreting his mild presence as a lack of strength and authority. They are, in effect, saying, "Paul is a nothing. He doesn't have

---

[1]  Buttrick, *The Interpreter's Bible,* Vol. IX, 383.

the presence of any leader we have ever seen. He talks a big talk when he is away but shrinks when he is here." His opposers have labeled Paul as being timid in their use of "meek," while Paul labels himself as "meek" in the sense of a quiet confidence in who he is in Christ.

If you are familiar with three of the most venerable theologians of the last few decades—Brennan Manning, Dallas Willard, and Eugene Peterson—consider their gentle and meek demeanor in the sense Paul is using here. Each of these men had a pronounced, relaxed presence about them. They didn't "put on airs," as some would say. Though each of them has written books that influenced millions, none of them had an attitude of superiority. They each came across as if they could have been the older next-door neighbor who spent his time tending the garden or sharing a glass of iced tea with you on a porch swing.

In a similar way, Paul's restraint is quite remarkable. In verse two of the passage above, he says he can indeed be stern if he needs to be; but he prefers to avoid doing so with his brothers and sisters in Christ. He urges them to not push him into using the world's tactics of boldness—the confidence of the flesh.

**"For though we live in the world, we do not wage war as the world does. The weapons we fight with are not the weapons of the world" (vv. 3–4a)**

This text is most often referenced as a passage about spiritual warfare. It certainly delivers on that point. But it is not a passage about how to deal with axe-bearing demoniacs. That type of evil is easy to recognize as demonic. The spiritual warfare Paul is talking about is more subtle. It is covert. It's the tendency for worldly influence to become the norm in the body of Christ. This is not about driving out demonic *possession*; it is about destroying demonic *influence*. The warfare Paul speaks of here is the war against the gospel and those who proclaim themselves as leaders of the church through the power of the flesh.

Paul is saying he refuses to practice authority through the power of the flesh, and he is placing fleshly, worldly authority in the category of spiritual powers in opposition to Christ's agenda. He declares that he has the authority to deal with troublemakers, but he doesn't need worldly weaponry and power to do so. He will not don Saul's armor. He refuses to use "means which appeal to human passions or lusts, as men do in a political struggle or in the competitive rivalries of business."[2] No, Paul does not find his authority in the power of the flesh but instead in the power of God. His weapons are not forged from human engineering but are divinely authored and given. The difference in these two forms comes from two different sources—the power of fleshly cunning versus the power of cross-bearing meekness.

The way of the cross—its apparent frailty—is contemptible and scandalous to the carnal mind. It is "foolishness to Gentiles" (1 Corinthians 1:23 NIV) and their way of thinking. This is no way to show power! Turn the other cheek? Bless your enemies? Assume the position of a servant rather than the master? Empty oneself of privilege rather than pack the heat of positional power? It is surely nonsense. The optics of the cross demonstrate weakness rather than strength in the eyes of the carnal onlooker, and yet the paradox of the kingdom stands: "The foolishness of God is wiser than human wisdom" (1 Corinthians 1:25 NIV).

Yes, we are indeed living in the natural world, but we are to be wiser than to wage battle on the world's terms. In the world of the spirit, human strength and intellectual constructs and systems are inferior and inadequate. Paul is declaring his refusal to use force or fleshly power even at the expense of appearing weak in others' eyes.

No aspect of the church and God's kingdom escapes the cruciform way. Leadership in Jesus' church must be formed, marked by, and occupied with daily cross-carrying. Its power lies in weakness. And anywhere the way of the cross is resisted is an issue of spiritual warfare. When Peter urged Jesus to resist the cross, the Lord spun around and

---

[2]  Ibid., 384.

shouted at him, "Get behind me, Satan!" (Matthew 16:23). Jesus exposed the demonic forces behind any resistance to the way of the cross.

**"On the contrary, they have divine power to demolish strongholds. We demolish arguments and every pretension that sets itself up against the knowledge of God, and we take captive every thought" (vv. 4b–5a)**

These fortresses or strongholds are, as the *King James Version* says, "imaginations, and every high thing" that have pitted themselves against the knowledge of God. When wrong thinking becomes systematized, it can develop into fortresses and strongholds of the mind that oppose the kingdom of God. And it is no trivial matter when those wrong ideologies form the institutions of the church. Spiritual warfare must be engaged against these strongholds of wrong ideology.

I must confess here that for me personally, challenging erroneous leadership systems in the church over the past dozen years has sometimes felt like a slog. I would much rather celebrate the joys of cotton candy and pony rides. Critics and even close friends have said, "You are always saying the bride is ugly." Other podcasters, bloggers, and authors speaking out about the leadership errors that have permeated the church have been accused of the same thing.

But what we are trying to say is not that Christ's bride is ugly, but that the behavior of Christ's groomsmen is ugly; not all of them by any means—but too many. It is ugly and abusive toward the bride and disrespectful toward Jesus, the bridegroom, to continue in the ways we have attended to the bride of Christ over the last few decades.

Any system of leadership is a system of power. They all assume the source of power, the intent of power, the distribution of power, and the rules of power. The warfare Paul is engaging here is against bastions built on the imaginations of people—worldly reasoning that has elevated paradigms and opinions to such a degree they have formed a power system in the name of the Lord that is actually a defense system *against* God.

**"To make it obedient to Christ" (v. 5b)**

Paul's ultimate intention is to cause the reasonings and opinions of people to be brought "captive to the *obedience* of Christ" (emphasis mine). He wants to break the powers of darkness.

The word Paul uses for "obedience" here is *hypakoē*, which means attentive hearing, or better yet, attentive thinking. It means to listen closely and obey what Jesus has said all along. When we blow off what Jesus said about leadership in his church—those little passages where he commanded us not to "exercise dominion" over one another, not to use rank-based titles that elevate some above their brothers and sisters in Christ, not to expect perks and privileges, not to seek to be first—we are patently ignoring Jesus. It is cognitive dissonance in its worst form. These are not preferences, nuances, or matters of choice in models or techniques. To ignore Jesus is not a minor issue. It is a matter of exalting our own imaginations, concepts, and ideas above the knowledge of God. It is to construct fortresses and castles against God's kingdom.

When we refuse to listen obediently to Jesus, we are not building his church; we are building our own kingdom. And it is a kingdom that is doomed.

> "Therefore, everyone who hears these words of Mine, and acts on them, will be like a wise man who built his house on the rock. And the rain fell and the floods came, and the winds blew and slammed against that house; and *yet* it did not fall, for it had been founded on the rock. And everyone who hears these words of Mine, and does not act on them, will be like a foolish man who built his house on the sand. And the rain fell and the floods came, and the winds blew and slammed against that house; and it fell—and its collapse was great."
>
> MATTHEW 7:24–27 NASB

For millennia, the prophets have called the people of God out on hearing but not listening and obeying. Hearing is the passive act of perceiving sound through our ears, whereas listening is the process of actively responding to what we've heard. Jeremiah confronted Israel's listening and obeying problem.

> "But this is what I commanded them, saying, 'Obey My voice, and I will be your God, and you will be My people; and you shall walk entirely in the way which I command you, so that it may go well for you.' Yet they did not obey or incline their ear, but walked by *their own* advice *and* in the stubbornness of their evil hearts, and they went backward and not forward."
>
> JEREMIAH 7:23-24 NASB

Obedient listening is a hallmark of our ongoing discipleship. Discipline and discipleship go hand in hand. Disciples add discipline to what they learn. A little side note is worth mentioning here. I find it interesting that the founder of chiropractic, D. D. Palmer, claimed his first patient had his hearing restored as a result of setting the atlas vertebra in order. The systemic effect of our present-day leadership constructs has certainly stifled the listening ear in the church today.

**"And we will be ready to punish every act of disobedience" (v. 6a)**
The Greek word for "disobedience" here is *parakoē*. It means inattention. Here we have the issue of listening again. Disobedience is inattentive hearing. The detractors think they are merely blowing Paul off and discrediting him. They say he is a nothing and not worth paying attention to. But they are actually not disobeying *Paul*. It is *Jesus* they are disobeying. The "disobedience" Paul is confronting here points back to verse 10:5—it is an issue of not obediently listening to Jesus.

Who would have thought that "not paying attention" could carry demonic overtones? Usually, when we think about inattention, we think of children who are easily distracted. "Pay attention," the teacher or parent says. But anyone who dares pick up the mantel of leadership and puts on a jersey with Jesus' name on the back has stepped into serious business. To disregard or give slack attention to what Jesus says puts both us and those we serve in serious peril.

This is not the only place Paul ties disobedience, or inattention to Jesus, to demonic influence:

> As for you, you were dead in your transgressions and sins, in which you used to live when you followed the ways of this world and of the ruler of the kingdom of the air, the spirit who is now at work in those who are disobedient. All of us also lived among them at one time, gratifying the cravings of our flesh and following its desires and thoughts.
>
> EPHESIANS 2:1–3 NIV

The key phrases—"ways of this world," "ruler of the kingdom of the air," "spirit who is now at work," "those who are disobedient," "cravings of our flesh," and "desires and thoughts"—summarize the source, the manifestation, and the hosts of demonic influence:

- Source: *ways of this world/ruler of the kingdom of the air/spirit who is now at work*
- Manifestation: *cravings of our flesh/desires and thoughts*
- Host: *those who are disobedient*

This is some hair-raising language. It reframes disobedience to Christ from being a neutral, freewill choice to a full-blown decision to draw from and align with the opposing forces of God's kingdom.

In his letter to the churches, the apostle James issues a stern warning:

> Who is wise and understanding among you? Let them show it by their good life, by deeds done in the humility that comes from wisdom. But if you harbor bitter envy and selfish ambition in your hearts, do not boast about it or deny the truth. Such "wisdom" does

not come down from heaven but is earthly, unspiritual, demonic. For
where you have envy and selfish ambition, there you find disorder
and every evil practice.

JAMES 3:13-16 NIV

Along with jealousy and arrogance, James calls out selfish ambition
(twice). He sarcastically calls it "wisdom." The *wisdom of the world,*
so often presented through leadership systems imported into the
church, is not "wisdom" for the saints—those commanded to not
be "of" the world. It is "foolishness in God's sight" (1 Corinthians
3:19 NIV). Accordingly, James points out the source of it all—base,
earthly, fleshly behavior. But above all, it is most terrifyingly demonic.
The ambition run amok in contemporary church leadership is not
merely banal or neutral in its origin. The apostle James agrees with
Paul that the underlying current here comes from the powers of
darkness.

In *The Scandal of Leadership*, missiologist JR Woodward says:

James points to *the source of false wisdom*, in that it comes from
below, it is "earthly, unspiritual, demonic" (3:15). James is now
linking envious desires to the work of the Powers. The effects
of a leader caught in the mimetic cycle are described by [Scot]
McKnight:

Those who are designed to follow Jesus, to live a life of loving
God and others, and to live out of the will of God are being
fractured into bits by teachers who abuse their authority, seek
to establish their reputations, and frame everything so as to
enlarge their own borders, and James knows that the messianic
community is at a crossroads. Either it gets back on track or
it will disintegrate into ineffective witness and missed opportunity. The options are two: either the teachers pursue a wisdom
that comes from God (see 3:17–18), or they continue on their
reckless, destructive path, which comes from Gehenna and the

evil spirit-world. Such a spirit-world distorts human community and institutionalizes injustices.[3]

### "Once your obedience is complete" (v. 6b)

The word Paul uses in 2 Corinthians 10:6 for "obedience" is again *hypakoē*, which means attentive listening. In essence, Paul is saying, "I want you to listen." The word for obedience here does not mean to *do* what I say. It means to *listen* to what I say. Those who have true confidence in their authority in Christ never demand blind allegiance and obeisance. They ask for a thoughtful hearing. Jesus frequently said, "Anyone with ears to hear should listen and understand" (Matthew 11:15 NLT). In the parable of the sower, Jesus mentions hearing and listening eight times, and he declares the parable is the key to understanding all his other parables. Obedience to Jesus can only come through thoughtfully listening to him, and it is the foundation of fruitfulness in everything the Lord teaches us.

*The Interpreter's Bible* says of 2 Corinthians,

> Two groups are here in mind. One is the church at Corinth as a whole; it is siding with the agitators who oppose Paul, and its obedience to Jesus is now far from complete. Since he uses spiritual methods, he cannot act against the real troublemakers until the majority take a favorable attitude toward him. As soon as they do, he can and will punish every disobedience of the active ringleaders.[4]

So, is Paul campaigning here? Is he waiting until he has won over the majority before he brings down the hammer of positional power on his enemies? Far from it. He is using wisdom. Earlier, we examined James' teachings on the wisdom that does not come from heaven. Here, Paul

---

[3]   JR Woodward, *The Scandal of Leadership: Unmasking the Powers of Domination in the Church* (Cody, WY: 100 Movements Publishing, 2023), 141–142, quoting Scot McKnight, *The Letter of James* (Grand Rapids, MI: Wm. B. Eerdmans Publishing Co., 2011), 308.

[4]   Buttrick, *The Interpreter's Bible*, Vol. IX, 385.

is using the wisdom that *does* come from heaven: "But the wisdom that comes from heaven is first of all pure; then peace-loving, considerate, submissive, full of mercy and good fruit, impartial and sincere" (James 3:17 NIV).

Paul demonstrates wise leadership by patiently waiting to win the hearts and minds of the church members—not to himself, but to obedience and loyalty to Jesus. He is giving them space for their own spiritual formation. It must be their decision to accept his guidance and his message. They must bring their thoughts into captive obedience.

Fleshly authority uses every available tool and tactic at its disposal to get its own way or agenda accomplished. But *spiritual authority* is counterintuitive. It lays down carnal tools and weaponry. Domineering leaders often use Hebrews 13:17 to justify and establish their own power: "Obey your leaders and submit *to them*" (emphasis mine). This seems clear enough, but it would be better to keep in mind the words of that great theologian, Inigo Montoya from the 1987 fairytale movie *The Princess Bride*: "You keep using that word. I do not think it means what you think it means."[5] The original hearers would have understood the Greek word that translates in English as "obey" much differently than we do because it means something very different. The word is not *hypakouō*, which means "to hearken to a command." It is also not *peitharcheō*, which means "to obey a superior." The word for "obey" in this verse is *peithō*, which means "to be persuaded by."

This is the key distinction between leadership authority in the kingdom of heaven and worldly leadership authority. Jesus' leaders do not "lord over" or dominate. Their potency is not in the power of their position; it is from the character of their disposition. They do not exercise power backed by an office or title. They walk in authority, backed by character. Godly servants, whose *fruit* is leadership, cause others to want to follow their lead because of who they are, not because of the position they hold. When one disagrees with a leader, if the

---

[5] *The Princess Bride*, directed by Rob Reiner (1987; United States, Act III Communications), VHS.

leader operates from heavenly wisdom, that leader gives patient space for mutual understanding. And if the one who is in opposition will listen, thoughts that need to be brought to obedience (persuaded by) are changed. This is a two-way street. A humble leader must be just as willing to listen to the other person as well. When there is mutual accountability, leadership shines brightest and yields the good fruit James promises.

**"So even if I boast somewhat freely about the authority the Lord gave us for building you up rather than tearing you down, I will not be ashamed of it" (v. 8)**
Here, Paul declares the ultimate intention of God-given authority: It is for building up the church. The phrase "building you up" is rendered as "edification" in several translations and is the same word Paul used in Ephesians 4:12 where he says the APEST gifts are given to build up or edify the body of Christ.

Paul goes on to say that if he were to choose to make an argument for his authority based on outward accomplishments, he could make a solid case for himself. In essence, Paul says, "If I played by my detractors' rules, I would *still* win the argument. I've got the experience and history to play the fleshly power game if I were to go that route." It is as if Paul is thinking, *I'm not going to boast in myself. But, boy, if I decided to boast, I sure could do some major-league boasting!*

Just imagine Paul sitting at his desk, pen in hand, looking at the paper in front of him—the letter he is writing. See him looking around, pondering—biting his lip, rubbing his jaw, fretting. He is torn. On one of Paul's shoulders is a little pink angel, transparent wings fluttering, pleading, "No, Paul. Stay humble. Don't brag about yourself." He yields, writing, "But, 'Let the one who boasts boast in the Lord.' For it is not the one who commends himself who is approved, but the one whom the Lord commends" (2 Corinthians 10:17–18 NIV).

But on Paul's other shoulder is a little red pitch-fork-carrying devil, whispering, "Brag on yourself. Tell 'em how important you are. Show your credentials. You are freaking Paul the apostle!" And it seems as if the more he thinks about it the more agitated he gets. So he scribbles, "I hope you will put up with me in a little foolishness" (2 Corinthians 11:1 NIV). Paul is about to go on a blistering diatribe. It's as if he says, "Crazy? You want to see crazy? I'll give you crazy!"

But that is not what is happening in Paul's head. Paul doesn't rely on his flesh for authority. He understands the source of spiritual authority. He knows where the power of God comes from. Yes, he will indeed boast. But he will boast not in his power but in his weakness. He will put the things the Corinthian Greeks considered foolishness— cross-bearing—on full display. He might be thinking, *You hate the foolishness of the cross, but you want a bold leader? I am a bold leader, but my boldness comes from meekness. You want power, but my power comes from weakness.*

Two other verses from 2 Corinthians are important to consider here: chapter 11, verses 6 and 15.

### "I may indeed be untrained as a speaker, but I do have knowledge" (v. 6)

Here Paul opens the argument for why he should be listened to. He declares that he is not inferior to his opponents, whom he calls "super-apostles"—a frothy sarcasm on his part. He also injects something very interesting at this point, saying, "I may indeed be untrained as a speaker, but I do have knowledge." It is hard for us to imagine it, but Paul may not have been as adept a speaker as we might assume. His speaking ability, or lack thereof, is a recurring theme. He already raised the fact that he had been criticized for this: "For some say, 'His letters are weighty and forceful, but in person he is unimpressive and his speaking amounts to nothing'" (2 Corinthians 10:10). "Paul doesn't carry himself as a great leader, and he is not a great speaker," his critics essentially said.

This is a significant point for us to consider. The Corinthians were Greeks. Grecian culture placed the utmost value upon oratory. They esteemed those who could give mesmerizing talks. The Greeks, through the influence of Gorgias of Sicily, Aristotle, Plato, Demosthenes, and others had created a culture that expected, yea demanded, astounding speeches from its leaders and great thinkers. You better bring your A-game in speaking if you were going to make it as a thought leader among the Greeks. The ones considered the greatest leaders were the greatest speakers. It went hand in hand.

Now we may think, *Yeah, but that was them.* But in the Western world, we are very "Greeky." In particular, the values and practices of Greek and Roman citizenship and politics, more than any other cultures, influence American policies today in terms of values, government, and self-image. They influenced our alphabet, language, entertainment, laws, architecture, religion, and calendar.[6] We think like the Greeks. The ones we place on the pedestal of leadership are the ones who can give pithy TED Talks, bring the house down in conferences, and command a room with riveting oratory. We are convinced that great leaders are the smartest ones in the room, and we believe they're the smartest because they speak the best. They can work a whiteboard with lightning-quick diagrams and points fired off from colored markers, and they write the books publishers know will sell. But Paul placed little weight on such skills:

> For Christ did not send me to baptize, but to preach the gospel, not with cleverness of speech, so that the cross of Christ would not be made of no effect.
>
> 1 CORINTHIANS 1:17 NASB

> When I came to you, brothers *and sisters,* I did not come as *someone* superior in speaking ability.
>
> 1 CORINTHIANS 2:1 NASB

> My message and my preaching were not with wise and persuasive

---

6  "The Greek and Roman Influence over Modern America," Bartleby.com, https://www.bartleby.com/essay/The-Greek-and-Roman-Influence-over-Modern-F32GJE9KRYZA.

words, but with a demonstration of the Spirit's power, so that your
faith might not rest on human wisdom, but on God's power.

1 CORINTHIANS 2:4–5 NIV

JR Woodward tells an interesting story about one of the most respected
influencers of the church over the last half-century. Dallas Willard
lectured philosophy for many years at the University of Southern
California, taught at Fuller Theological Seminary, and authored many
best-selling books, including *The Spirit of the Disciplines* and *The
Divine Conspiracy*. Woodward recounts one particular interaction he
had with Willard:

> Our network once invited him to speak at our conference. I happened
> to be the host of the particular session in which Dallas was to speak.
> It was my responsibility to lead a question-and-answer time after
> his talk. Just before I went up, I felt the Spirit leading me to say
> something I didn't want to say because I thought it might embarrass
> Dallas. So I rejected what I sensed to be the Spirit's prompting. Then
> I sensed the Spirit prompt me once more, just before I got up. So I
> stood beside Dallas and said what came to my mind.
>
> "Dallas, I've noticed that you are not a good speaker," I said.
> "You're not a charismatic speaker. You speak with a monotone voice.
> You are just not an impressive speaker."
>
> I could sense the uneasiness of the audience and noticed a few
> raised eyebrows. They must have been thinking, *What in the world
> is JR doing?*
>
> Despite this, I continued. "But then I noticed something else.
> When you were speaking, everyone was on the edge of their seat, just
> waiting for the next word to drop from your mouth."
>
> He patted me on my shoulder, as if to comfort me. He nodded
> his head during the entire time I was nervously talking; and in the
> midst of the awkward laughter of the crowd, he shared how he
> purposely chose not to use the common tactics that speakers use,
> because he wanted people to see God's power at work through him.

Dallas did indeed have a presence about him, a power and authority that was not his own.

Willard wrote several books, many on discipleship, but never once did he write a book proposal. He never sought to put himself forward. He only responded to requests that publishers made of him. Dallas has been an example to me and many others, and he embodied what it means to be an example in the way of Christ. He was a kenotic leader who resisted the principalities of image, institution, and ideology.[7]

Dallas Willard was like Paul in this regard. Paul's confidence was in true God-given power—the spiritual authority from God, not the fleshly skill of humanity.

### "[Satan's] servants also masquerade as servants of righteousness" (v. 15)

Paul moves on to distinguish other vital differences between a worldly leadership persona and true spiritual authority. He reminds the Corinthians that he did not demand special treatment and that he labored among them at no charge, so he was not a burden to them, financially or otherwise. Then Paul calls out the ways of the super-apostles who had gained influence over the Corinthian church:

> For such people are false apostles, deceitful workers, masquerading as apostles of Christ. And no wonder, for Satan himself masquerades as an angel of light. It is not surprising, then, if his servants also masquerade as servants of righteousness. Their end will be what their actions deserve.
>
> 2 CORINTHIANS 11:13–15 NIV

They masquerade as apostles of Christ and "servants of righteousness," Paul says, but their deeds show they are anything but servants. In the

---

7    Woodward, *The Scandal of Leadership*, 209.

streams of today's church, this plays out in different ways. Over the years, there have been pastors and faith-based organizational leaders who have been exposed for extravagant living, misappropriation of funds, and even embezzlement. In many "prosperity gospel" circles, it seems as if greed for material things and money is explicit—even flaunted. I remember watching televangelist Jesse Duplantis boasting that he owns the biggest house in the state of Louisiana. He is also the one who pressed his followers to fund a new $58 million jet for his "ministry."[8] A Missouri-based pastor was rightly criticized for going on a tirade against his church for not honoring him by buying him a luxury watch he had said he wanted.[9]

Leaders who demand privileges are plainly not servants—which is the first requirement and measurement for following Jesus, let alone those leading in his name. Those who carry on in such a way not only expose themselves, but they also disqualify themselves from leadership and scandalize the church to a watching world.

Paul continues his brilliant play on words, again mixed with sarcasm:

> Since many are boasting in the way the world does, I too will boast. You gladly put up with fools since you are so wise! In fact, you even put up with anyone who enslaves you or exploits you or takes advantage of you or puts on airs or slaps you in the face. To my shame I admit that we were too weak for that!
>
> 2 CORINTHIANS 11:18–21 NIV

Paul sarcastically retorts, "Shame on me! I am certainly weak when compared to those who abuse you." The false apostles (11:13), those with so-called *authority*, have been slave masters of the Corinthian

---

[8] jeschneiderx (@jeschneiderx), "Jesse Duplantis—I Am Living At The Top," TikTok, accessed July 27, 2023, https://www.tiktok.com/@jeschneiderx/video/7215304750177242411.

[9] Natalie O'Neill, "'False prophet' pastor berates congregation for not buying him pricey new watch," *New York Post*, August 17, 2022, https://nypost.com/2022/08/17/missouri-pastor-berates-congregation-for-not-buying-him-new-watch/.

church. They have dominated and used the sheep. Ezekiel's prophecy against the shepherds of Israel is apt: "With force and harshness you have ruled" (Ezekiel 34:4) the weakened flock. What these false leaders boast about and criticize Paul for *not* doing is not the way of the Lord. It is not spiritual authority. It is carnal, false power, manifesting as domination and false service. Likewise, the "apostles" undermining Paul present themselves in a superior posture. And it appears normal to the Corinthian, Greek-thinking church. They think this is what a leader looks like. This is how one with real authority does their job.

This is the case today in so many streams of the evangelical church. In recent years, many famous and revered pastors of huge churches and ministries have been exposed as operating with arrogant and domineering tactics that abuse staff members, young interns, and volunteers. And they get away with it, at least for a time, because people think it is normal. It is what a powerful leader looks like. People are fearful of losing employment or missing out on something that seems to be great.

So, Paul says, "Yes, I'm a weak leader, compared to *those* leaders." But Paul continues to boast in his weakness: He tells of the beatings and stonings he endured, the lashings he took, the shipwrecks he survived, floating in the open sea. He recounts his imprisonments and the dangers he faced on his journeys of proclaiming the gospel—including threats from robbers, false brethren, and fellow countrymen. He recounts times of starvation and exposure to the elements. On top of it all he mentions his heartfelt anxiety for the state of the churches.[10]

Again, incline your ear to what Paul is saying. This section of his letter all began with the argument that Paul was weak; that he was not bold; that he didn't act or speak like a *leader;* that he didn't really have authority. But now he has indeed turned to boasting—though not in the way humans boast—pointing out their accolades, titles, demands, and positions. Paul says, "If I must boast, I will boast of the things that show my weakness" (2 Corinthians 11:30 NIV).

---

[10]  See 2 Corinthians 11:23–29.

But that very weakness is the secret of his strength, his spiritual authority.

> But he said to me, "My grace is sufficient for you, for my power is made perfect in weakness." Therefore I will boast all the more gladly about my weaknesses, so that Christ's power may rest on me. That is why, for Christ's sake, I delight in weaknesses, in insults, in hardships, in persecutions, in difficulties. For when I am weak, then I am strong.
>
> 2 CORINTHIANS 12:9–10 NIV

This passage begins with a remarkable point we must not miss. Paul reveals a kingdom key about human power and what it takes to bring it into submission to God's power. If we want to see the power and strength of the Lord's leadership and authority, we must abandon our own power and strength. Jesus has been given "all rule and authority and power and dominion" and is "head over all" (Ephesians 1:20–22). There is no room for two heads in the body of Christ. Jesus is either the Head of your church or he's not. No mixture is permissible.

## THE END OF *OUR* POWER, THE BEGINNING OF HIS

The remarkable theologian Marva Dawn provides an insightful exegesis of Paul's statement, "But he said to me, 'My grace is sufficient for you, for my power is made perfect in weakness'" (2 Corinthians 12:9). Her research reveals the verb *teleō* is mistranslated as "made perfect" and should be translated as "brought to an end." She also notes,

> The Greek text of 2 Corinthians 12:9 contains no pronoun in connection with *hē dunamis*, "the power." Interpreting the power as Paul's rather than God's leads to significantly different theological

conclusions that are very important here for our discussion of being Church in a world characterized by the workings of various principalities and powers.[11]

In other words, when Paul says that God told him *his* grace was sufficient and he follows by saying, "*My* power is made perfect in weakness," the "my power" refers not to God's power but to Paul's power. Paul's statement should be rendered, "And he had said to me, 'My (God's) grace is sufficient for you.' For my (Paul's) power is *brought to an end* in weakness." Paul is saying that by choosing to embrace—rather than resist—weakness, he can subdue the use of his own fleshly power, and thus make room for God's power.

When we come to the end of our own methods—of cunning, worldly wisdom, and strength—we make way for God's ways, wisdom, and spiritual authority—his grace—to work through us. "For the mind that is set on the flesh is hostile to God, for it does not submit to God's law; indeed, it cannot" (Romans 8:7). The reason this is an issue of spiritual warfare is because the powers of darkness seek to usurp the throne of God. And they use methods of domination to do so. Those methods are based on carnality. They are ultimately futile in bringing us into the genuine authority God's kingdom offers.

The kingdom Jesus establishes is truly foolish-looking. Jesus not only comes on the scene as a helpless infant, but he also rides into Jerusalem for his Passion on a baby donkey instead of a stallion. Have you ever considered how foolish a grown man looks on a little donkey? Before being arrested and tortured, Jesus tells Peter he has the power to call down legions of angels to intervene, but he lays down that privilege. Jesus then defeats the powers of darkness by giving himself up, hanging naked on a cross. He instructs both the crowds in public and his disciples in private to follow the ways of little children and servants, not kings and conquerors. Those at the "top" spiritually

---

[11] Marva J. Dawn, *Powers, Weakness and the Tabernacling of God* (Grand Rapids, MI: Wm. B. Eerdmans Publishing Co., 2001), 38.

position themselves at the bottom when it concerns their own flesh and what it offers.

Authentic spiritual authority is needed in the church today as much as ever. But it is counterintuitive by almost any measure. The subversive paradox of non-authoritarian authority is a key to the kingdom of heaven's way of leadership. The adoption of worldly "wisdom" has caused the church to become enmeshed with the powers of darkness. We have sown to the wind and reaped the whirlwind of scandal and bondage. In doing so, we have forfeited the true spiritual authority of God and paralyzed the body of Christ. May we repent and realign to our true Atlas—Jesus, the Head of his Church.

## For Teams to Process

- Are we relying on our own strength and wisdom in leading the church, or are we truly submitting to God's grace and authority?
- In what ways might our leadership be influenced by worldly wisdom or carnal power, rather than rooted in the servant-leadership modeled by Jesus?
- How does the concept of "power made perfect in weakness" manifest in our personal lives and leadership styles?
- Do we view authority in the church as a platform for domination or as a responsibility to shepherd and serve the congregation?
- Are our church's methods and strategies aligned with the kingdom principles of grace, humility, and spiritual authority?
- In moments of difficulty or conflict, do we resort

to fleshly methods to resolve issues, or do we seek divine guidance and grace?

- What steps can we take to foster an environment where the true spiritual authority of God can flourish within our church community?
- How often do we consider the implications of spiritual warfare in the choices we make and actions we take as leaders in the church?
- In what ways might our church be enmeshed with the "powers of darkness" due to the adoption of worldly wisdom?
- How can we collectively repent and realign our focus to ensure that Jesus is the true Head of this church, embracing his counterintuitive methods of authority?

# 5

# HEAD OF A FAMILY

## Realigning as a Household of Faith

*We have a need to belong because belonging is really a*
*"longing to be." It is a longing to be who we are created to be.*
*It is a longing to be with those who know us and love us, and*
*ultimately it is a longing to be with our heavenly Father.*

ROBERT FRYLING

It was lunchtime for us eighth graders. As a few of us were just about to dig into our meal of Sloppy Joes and French fries, I glanced across the table and noticed that Ross and Kip Clawson each had a spattering of red dots all over their faces. The Clawson brothers were inseparable. Ross was a year older than Kip but had been held back a grade. I always figured he had failed third grade on purpose, so he could hang back with Kip. "What happened to you guys? Do ya'll have chicken pox?" I asked. "He-he," Ross chuckled, grinning at Kip. He looked back at me, "Us and Daddy had a pellet-gun fight last night. In the house! Ha ha!" They both laughed uproariously, and Kip slapped the table.

It turned out that, at some point, two of the brothers—there was a third (older) brother—had swapped insults, and within seconds all four male members of the Clawson clan were seeking cover behind sofas, chairs, and around hallway corners, blasting away at one another with pellet guns. In the house!

From this brief story, you can already tell that the Clawsons were ... let's just say, *different*. They were a rowdy bunch. They would fight with one another not only with fists but also with firearms. Ross and Kip were always pounding on one another, and they frequently had bruises and black eyes as evidence of the riotous relationships in their family. Despite their willingness to pounce on one another, there was one thing everyone knew: You dare not strike a Clawson brother, or you risked facing all the other siblings. They always stuck together. Their loyalty was the upside of their family dynamic.

The downside was their dysfunctional and harmful way of dealing with conflict. Being part of a family is often traumatic. For some people, hearing church folk say, "Welcome to the family," triggers that trauma. And for too many, their fears are realized after settling in.

## METAPHORS MATTER

In chapter three, we looked at the metaphor of Christ as the Head of his body, the church. And in chapter four, we saw that the headship of Christ isn't just semantics; it is spiritual warfare. But, in the New Testament, Christ's headship carries a double meaning, underscored by metaphors of both *body* and *family*. Jesus is the Head of the body, and he is the Head of the family. The church is constantly referred to as a family in Scripture. The term for brethren, which connotes fellow believers (including females) is used more than 250 times in the context of church-family relationships from the book of Acts onward. Both Peter and Paul used the term "household" as a descriptor of the church. "Household" is the Greek word οἰκεῖος. It means: "belonging to a house or family, domestic, intimate: related by blood, kindred."[1] We see this time after time, as I've emphasized in the verses below:

---

[1] James Strong, *Strong's Exhaustive Concordance of the Bible: With Greek and Hebrew Dictionaries* (Gordonsville, TN: Dugan Publishers, 1984), s.v. "household."

So then, while we have opportunity, let's do good to all people, and especially to those who are of the **household** of faith.

GALATIANS 6:10 NASB

So then you are no longer strangers and foreigners, but you are fellow citizens with the saints, and are of God's **household**.

EPHESIANS 2:19 NASB

*I write* so that you will know how one should act in the **household** of God, which is the church of the living God, the pillar and support of the truth.

1 TIMOTHY 3:15 NASB

For *it is* time for judgment to begin with the **household** of God; and if *it begins* with us first, what *will be* the outcome for those who do not obey the gospel of God?

1 PETER 4:17 NASB

Writing on the "church as a loving family," Australian theologian and church planter Robert Banks says,

Most of the words Paul employs come from the intimate side of family affairs. *Adelphoi*, "brethren," is far and away Paul's favorite way of referring to the members of the communities to whom he is writing. This word is often used generically of both males and females, as the word "folks" is used in American English. In spite of its frequency and its more limited reference to those who are colleagues in Paul's mission, the term "brethren" has not yet lost its basic meaning and become a mere formal description. There are many passages in Paul's writings where it is clearly expressive of the real relationship that exists between Christians, not least when they come together as church.[2]

---

[2] Robert J. Banks, *Paul's Idea of Community: The Early House Churches in Their Cultural Setting*, rev. ed. (Peabody, MA: Hendrickson Publishers, 1994), 50–51.

Banks's point is underscored as we read more from Paul:

> Therefore, I urge you, brothers and sisters, in view of God's mercy, to offer your bodies as a living sacrifice, holy and pleasing to God—this is your true and proper worship.
>
> ROMANS 12:1 NIV

> For through your knowledge the one who is weak is ruined, the brother *or sister* for whose sake Christ died. And so, by sinning against the brothers *and sisters* and wounding their conscience when it is weak, you sin against Christ. Therefore, if food causes my brother to sin, I will never eat meat again, so that I will not cause my brother to sin.
>
> 1 CORINTHIANS 8:11–13 NASB

> You, my brothers and sisters, were called to be free. But do not use your freedom to indulge the flesh; rather, serve one another humbly in love.
>
> GALATIANS 5:13 NIV

> And because of my chains, most of the brothers and sisters have become confident in the Lord and dare all the more to proclaim the gospel without fear.
>
> PHILIPPIANS 1:14 NIV

Those passages are but a small sampling of the abundance of familial language used throughout the New Testament by both Jesus and the writers.

## FAMILIES ARE MESSY—YET ...

No one grows up in a perfect family. The portrayals of idyllic families of the early television era are just that—portrayals. Fiction. Though some of us grew up with mostly good experiences in our families, sadly, many people suffer lifelong pain and trauma because of family relationships. When some of us hear the term "family," the first things that come to mind are domination, abuse, and control—the very things this book is seeking to move us away from. While acknowledging that the analogy of family is difficult for some, we still see that the biblical metaphor of family centers on God's best intention and idea for families. The last place anyone should experience trauma and abuse is the family. The Lord's idea of family is that it should be the safest, most inclusive, most encouraging, and most hope-building unit we could possibly be a part of.

The "one another" passages found throughout the New Testament teach believers how to relate to one another as family. Blogger Jeffy Crantz points out that about 15 percent of these passages stress an attitude of humility and deference.[3]

1. Wash one another's feet (John 13:14)
2. Give preference to one another in honor (Romans 12:10)
3. Don't be haughty: be of the same mind (Romans 12:16)
4. Serve one another (Galatians 5:13)
5. Be subject to one another (Ephesians 5:21)
6. Regard one another as more important than yourselves (Philippians 2:3)
7. Clothe yourselves in humility toward one another (1 Peter 5:5)

These instructions are not nullified for church staff. Senior leaders do not get leadership immunity from obeying these commands. In fact, according to Jesus, the *greatest* among us are the ones who shine the brightest in obeying such instructions.

The body of Christ is a family, and when we think of our church staff, the principle of "like produces like" applies. If our staff doesn't operate as a family, our church will not have the culture of a family. Sure, we can talk family talk, but talk can be void of actual substance—like

---

[3] Jeffrey Kranz, "All the 'one another' commands in the NT [infographic]," March 9, 2014, https://overviewbible.com/one-another-infographic/.

a hollow chocolate bunny. You bite into it and there is nothing but air. If our church staff operates as a corporate entity, so will our churches.

We can apply all the catchphrases we want in our marketing pieces and on Sunday mornings, but if our staff is not family, nobody is family. Orange trees don't produce apples. If the teams that lead our churches operate like a typical business, we are merely offering religious goods and services to religious consumers. I am confident that none of us really wants that.

A strong argument can be made that the intimacy of family affection is the overriding theme in the epistles. Writing to the Thessalonian church, Paul prays, "May the Lord make you increase and abound in love for one another" (1 Thessalonians 3:12). In his first letter to the Corinthian church, he urges, "I appeal to you, brothers and sisters, in the name of our Lord Jesus Christ, that all of you agree with one another in what you say and that there be no divisions among you, but that you be perfectly united in mind and thought" (1 Corinthians 1:10 NIV). These words are not intended to be flowery prose. They are instructional pathways to becoming what we are meant to be as the family of God.

It would be inconceivable for the writers of the New Testament to imagine a church where many families leave a Sunday morning service to drive costly vehicles to sit down for expensive restaurant meals … while a single mom rises from the same row of chairs to drive her kids home in a car billowing black smoke, worrying about whether she can afford to feed her family the upcoming week. I am convinced that Paul would have brought correction if such a scenario had taken place in one of the churches.

It is our tangible love for one another that marks us as the family of God. Using the "one another" phrase so many times and in so many ways makes Scripture a tangible, practical matter for us all. The actions that love produces make the body of Christ healthy and whole. It was what was so appealing about the church in its earliest days. The contemporary church has replaced practical love with the latest evangelistic method, program, or technique. We have stopped producing the attractional fragrance of love for one another that causes a watching world to seek us out. The greatest appeal of the church should not be its cutting-edge worship services and great preaching; it should be tangible love lived out in a genuine community.

Our connection to one another as brothers and sisters—as disciples of Jesus—is the true love connection that causes a watching world to see him in our midst: "By this all people will know that you are my disciples, if you have love for one another" (John 13:35).

## SIBLINGS WITHOUT RIVALRY

To our detriment, we have replaced the family analogies used by the New Testament writers with others we prefer. And it's worth noting that the Holy Spirit inspired the writers to use the words they did. I believe it is fair to ask if our replacement terms have caused us to conflict with the Holy Spirit's leading. The issue here is far weightier than semantics. This is not about whether you say "to-may-to" or "to-mah-to."

Some terms carry a relational component to them, and some do not. Certain words evoke intimacy or boundaries. If I call someone my "coach," I'm conveying that they are someone who watches as I carry out a task or activity and instructs me on how to perform better. That may be all there is to the relationship. But if I call someone my "mentor," I imply something more intimate. They may be a coach, a player, or expert, but they are also pouring experiential wisdom into me. Calling them my mentor tells you a deeper relationship exists. All mentors are coaches, but all coaches are not mentors. Words matter.

So how should we refer to one another within the culture of church staff? Along with the expressions of "fellow workers," we see sibling terms used repeatedly throughout the scriptural code. Notice in the passage we looked at earlier (Matthew 23:8), where Jesus forbids rank-based titles, he gives the underlying reason behind the command: "[because] you are all brothers and sisters." We are siblings in the Lord. This is the relational component of his kingdom, and it never goes away. It is not to be circumvented. Regardless of any vocational position we might hold, in the church we have the same Father. The only honest justification for using business terms is to admit we do indeed view the church as a business structured by hierarchy. By the way, if you look up the terms "hireling" and "employee" in Greek and English dictionaries, they both have the same definition. Men and women who have responded to God's call on their lives to serve in vocational roles on church staff are not "employees." They are not "hirelings." They are fellow servants.

As we explored in chapter one, in 1 Samuel 8, when the people of Israel demanded to have a king over them, the Lord gave in to their demands. Speaking through the prophet Samuel, the first thing God had to say about it was that they were rejecting their true King. God was enough, but the people wouldn't have it. They were not connected intimately enough with God to know that God was more than enough. And they wanted a human to deliver the goods of intimacy with God without having to do the work on their own.

Long before this, the Lord prophesied this would take place. Predicting a time when Israel would demand a king for a leader, God gave strict instructions for how that person should live so that *"his heart may not be lifted up above his brothers*, and that he may not turn aside from the commandment" (Deuteronomy 17:20, emphasis mine). This is the way of kings. They believe they are better than others. Their hearts become puffed up and lifted above their brothers and sisters. They no longer view those below them—and everyone *is* below them—as siblings. Yet, in the kingdom of God, we are all brothers and sisters, under one Father. And our Father is the King.

The essence of our relationship with God as Father is conveyed when Paul writes, "And because we are his children, God has sent the Spirit of his Son into our hearts, prompting us to call out, 'Abba, Father'" (Galatians 4:6 NLT). Eugene Peterson's translation in *The Message* phrases this verse so well: "You can tell for sure that you are now fully adopted as his own children because God sent the Spirit of his Son into our lives crying out, 'Papa! Father!'"

Most importantly, it is Jesus himself who uses the language of family to describe his true followers: "And looking about at those who sat around Him, He said, 'Here are my mother and my brothers! For whoever does the will of God, he is my brother, and sister, and mother'" (Mark 3:34–35).

The terminology used in the New Testament allows no place for referring to others as employees or employers. A boss/employee relationship is based on an exchange. We trade time for money. I agree to work for you if you will give me a certain sum of currency. If you are my boss, I answer directly and firstly to you.

When the church meets or a church staff comes together, it is not a gathering of club members or employees. It is not analogous to Jeff Bezos calling for a meeting in the conference room. It is the family coming to the dining room with Jesus at the head of the table. The language, terms, and titles we use within this context have a significant impact on forming the culture. Borrowing terminology from the business world has formed a corporate culture in too many churches and faith-based organizations today. It makes vendors of religious goods and services out of leaders, and creates consumers out of Christians. It's a lower way.

> "Ah, stubborn children," declares the Lord, "who carry out a plan, but not mine, and who make an alliance, but not of my Spirit, that they may add sin to sin; who set out to go down to Egypt, without asking for my direction, to take refuge in the protection of Pharaoh and to seek shelter in the shadow of Egypt!"
>
> ISAIAH 30:1–2

Egypt represents the way of the world. It is a fallen and dark kingdom. It is a lower way. It is a pseudo way. This is why the prophets would so often use the phrase "go *down* into Egypt."[4] In the passage above, the Lord accuses the nation of Israel of being stubborn children who make an alliance with the kingdom of darkness. It was not a higher way, but a lower way.

---

4   See also Gen 46:3, Deut 26:5, and Isa 52:4, for example.

## FAMILY RESTORATION

Paul seasons our thinking with familial language regarding many issues. In the last part of his letter to the church in Galatia, he says,

> Brothers *and sisters*, even if a person is caught in any wrongdoing, you who are spiritual are to restore such a person in a spirit of gentleness; *each one* looking to yourself, so that you are not tempted as well. Bear one another's burdens, and thereby fulfill the law of Christ ... So then, while we have opportunity, let's do good to all people, and especially to those who are of the household of the faith.
>
> GALATIANS 6:1–2 10 NASB

He is telling us (and the Clawson brothers!), "Don't shoot at each other. You are brothers and sisters. When one of you falls through sin or stumbles under the load of life, act like the family that you are and restore the individual."

When we hear of either a national or local leader who has been caught in wrongdoing, we often hear that they are going to be placed in a "process of restoration." Or sometimes the process is referred to as "church discipline." However, these terms rarely mean that a local church family of everyday brethren is walking the church leader back to spiritual or emotional health. It usually means an outside firm or agency is intervening, with the church leader removed from the fellowship for a period, or permanently, to journey through some program. But Paul commands those who "are spiritual" *among* the brothers and sisters to do the restoring.

Instead of immediately outsourcing or institutionalizing restoration, we should function as the family of God and follow Jesus' restoration process found in Matthew 18.

> "If your brother or sister sins, go and point out their fault, just between the two of you. If they listen to you, you have won them over. But if they will not listen, take one or two others along, so that 'every matter may be established by the testimony of two or three

witnesses.' If they still refuse to listen, tell it to the church; and if they refuse to listen even to the church, treat them as you would a pagan or a tax collector."

MATTHEW 18:15–17 NIV

When we have problems among our natural family members, if we are functioning healthily, we don't immediately cast them out or ship them off somewhere. We look to resolve the problems with each other. If those problems are more severe than we can handle ourselves, we get some outside help, either from friends or family counseling. But we are still working together as a family for healing and unity. If the problems involve abuses in the family, outside help is essential. We need trained professionals to keep people safe, work through past traumas, and move us toward future health. Sometimes the abuse is so severe that temporary separation is necessary unless it is determined that permanent separation is the only option. But safety, unity, healing, and restoration are always the goals in Jesus' plan of family restoration. The same processes should and can be done in God's church family. The New Testament writers emphasize that being equipped for such a task should be the norm for the family of God, and we are at fault for not meeting this expectation.

When was the last time you heard of a fallen pastor remaining in the church as a member, under submission to a process of restoration led by fellow church members? Under our current leadership systems, this is untenable. The pastor has been the one with all the authority. They are not a sibling; they are our leader. They have not been *among* us; they have been *over* us. The familial relationship is nonexistent. Misalignment to Jesus, the true Atlas of the body, means that the only option is to banish the fallen leader or send them to professionals to get fixed.

Some people might argue, "But we are not *all* siblings! What about the spiritual fathers and mothers in the family of God?" They point to passages such as 1 Timothy 5:1 and 1 Timothy 1:2, where Paul calls Timothy "his son," as well as when Paul calls himself a "father in Christ" and the Corinthian believers his "beloved children" in 1 Corinthians 4:14–15. But that would be taking those few words completely out of context. Paul does use those terms, but only after calling them "brothers and sisters" and strongly rebuking them for their error of lifting up certain leaders above themselves:

> For when one says, "I follow Paul," and another, "I follow Apollos," are you not mere human beings? What, after all, is Apollos? And what is Paul? Only servants, through whom you came to believe—as the Lord has assigned to each his task ... So then, no more boasting about human leaders! All things are yours, whether Paul or Apollos or Cephas or the world or life or death or the present or the future— all are yours, and you are of Christ, and Christ is of God.
>
> 1 CORINTHIANS 3:4–5, 21–23 NIV

When Paul calls the Corinthians "children," he's actually saying, "Don't act like children by trying to lift up someone above you!"

> Brothers and sisters, I could not address you as people who live by the Spirit but as people who are still worldly—mere infants in Christ. I gave you milk, not solid food, for you were not yet ready for it. Indeed, you are still not ready.
>
> 1 CORINTHIANS 3:1–2 NIV

And when he reminds them he is their "father in Christ," in essence, he is saying, "If anyone could claim to be your 'father,' it's me because you came to know Christ first through my preaching. But don't do that! Don't lift anyone above yourself."

As for when Paul refers to Timothy as "son," Paul is again referencing how Timothy first came to faith through Paul; so, in a way, Paul was Timothy's "spiritual father." However, Paul refers to Timothy as a "brother" much more often in Scripture than he does a "son" (2 Corinthians 1:1; Colossians 1:1; 1 Thessalonians 3:2; Hebrews 13:23). If "spiritual parenthood" is a thing, then it should be a temporary situation, not ongoing paternalism. We are all "siblings," and none of us can claim the role of "mother" or "father" other than God.

Paul places a ton of responsibility on the family of God to care for one another. There are more than one hundred instances in the New Testament where we are given instruction about relationships with "one another." Like a team of carpenters driving one nail after another, the writers of the epistles use the term as a command over and over: Serve one another—*bam!* Be devoted to one another—*bam!* Speak the truth to one another—*bam!* Be subject to one another—*bam!* Confess your sins to one another—*bam!*[5] It goes on and on.

## A TRUE STORY[6]

After two decades as a pastor, Kevin came to the place where his greatest passion was church planting. The church he had founded years earlier helped to plant several others, and more and more of his time and enthusiasm was aimed toward coaching others to start churches. He ended up accepting a position as church-planting director for a large church that was prolific in starting churches. He loved the new role. It was as if this was what he was made for—spending every day working with young men and women, helping to equip, resource, train, and mentor them to go to cities around America and other nations to start churches.

Kevin's office was situated near the offices of two incredibly gifted women who each led missional initiatives, as well as the office of another wonderful leader who focused on global and local mission. Their collective experience, knowledge, and insight was substantial. They each had trained and helped many church members discover their own giftings and brought them onto their teams. Over the past year, all four leaders had witnessed exponential growth in the minis-tries they were overseeing.

---

[5] Gal 5:13, Rom 12:10, Eph 4:25, Eph 5:21, Jas 5:16.

[6] The names in this story have been changed to protect the privacy of individuals.

The four team members collaborated, prayed together, encouraged one another, and sharpened each other. The cross-pollination of their collective wisdom, experience, and giftings created a synergy that benefitted the whole church. Their combined efforts and giftings seeped into most areas of the church, and the church not only grew in health but also saw tangible kingdom impact.

As with any family, things could have been better. They could have operated with much less stress, more speed, and more day-to-day joy. But their primary dysfunction arose from the leadership system—the structure. As has become the prevailing norm in so many contemporary churches, Kevin's church had installed an executive pastor, Rex, whose job was to manage everything *below* the senior pastor. Coming from the corporate business world with expertise in marketing, Rex had no pastoral or church-planting leadership experience. Nevertheless, he had been appointed as boss over all four veterans and outlined their schedules and permissions for what they could and could not do. Because … that's what management does.

Thankfully, Rex was not a jerk. He was a wonderful guy who was personable and deeply loved Jesus and the church. The problem— as with many who operate in positions as executive pastors—was the modus operandi itself. It was incongruous with the family of Jesus. This executive pastor would have been enormously helpful as a coach and equipper; and when he functioned in those lanes, he strengthened the entire staff. Rex's brilliance and capacity for organizing were world-class. He asked great questions and helped the team consider details they often would have missed because they were not wired like him. However, instead of treating his co-staff like brothers and sisters, the worldly paradigm of his role as executive director led him to "lord over" the team and use domination tactics. The issue was systemic and structural. Jesus explicitly forbade this approach among his disciples.

A dispute also arose among them, as to which of them was to be regarded as the greatest. And he said to them, "The kings of the

Gentiles exercise lordship over them, and those in authority over them are called benefactors. But not so with you. Rather, let the greatest among you become as the youngest, and the leader as one who serves."

LUKE 22:24–26

Author Frank Viola comments on the contrasts in hierarchical leadership emanating from the systems of the world with what Jesus calls us to as his family, operating as citizens of his kingdom:

- In the Gentile world, leaders operate on the basis of a political, chain-of-command social structure—a graded hierarchy. In the kingdom of God, leadership flows from childlike meekness and sacrificial service.
- In the Gentile world, authority is based on position and rank. In the kingdom of God, authority is based on godly character. Note Christ's description of a leader "let the greatest among you become as the youngest, and the leader as one who serves." In our Lord's eyes, *being* precedes *doing*. And *doing* flows from *being*. Put differently, function follows character. Those who serve do so because they *are* servants.
- In the Gentile world, greatness is measured by prominence, external power, and political influence. In the kingdom of God, greatness is measured by humility and servitude.
- In the Gentile world, leaders exploit their positions to rule over others. In the kingdom of God, leaders deplore special reverence. They rather regard themselves "as the younger."[7]

In Kevin's situation, the executive pastor was a classic upper manager. That was his background. It was as if he had management contact lenses and couldn't see any other way of leading. Each one of the

---

[7] Frank Viola, *Reimagining Church: Pursuing the Dream of Organic Christianity* (Colorado Springs, Co: David C. Cook, 2008), 157.

seasoned men and women on the team had to ask his permission—not his counsel—for how to go about their duties. And way too often they were rebuffed because the executive pastor wanted them at the mother church, even though much of their work was in the field.

As a developer of young church planters, Kevin needed to spend a lot of time with men and women who were starting churches across a large metropolitan area. One of the best experiences he could give his mentees was to take them to fledgling churches to visit their services and spend time with their pastors. But Kevin was only allowed a few Sundays to do so. Rex wanted Kevin and his trainees "at home" for 90 percent of Sundays. It didn't matter that the church held a weekly Saturday evening service they all could attend to stay connected with the direction of the mother church. This was the way it was to be. Rex was the boss and had the final say.

Despite his relative lack of insight and involvement in each ministry area, Rex had veto power over every sphere. And he established the rules. Although Kevin and the team had more collective experience in their ministry area, he outranked them and therefore they had to do things his way. This system not only immobilized the team and the wider church family from advancing in greater and speedier ways, but it also zapped creativity, enthusiasm, and joy from team members, who all experienced the same levels of command-and-control management.

As their ministries grew, the senior pastor and executive pastor decided the missions department needed more management. Was it because they were stalled or stumbling? Far from it; they were hitting on all cylinders. But this is what a management-minded organization does. It adds more layers of management. Kevin was approached three times about being elevated to senior director over the other three team members. Though it would have meant more pay and status, he turned it down every time. Kevin told the senior pastor they didn't need another layer of management and that they were being over-managed as it was. His opinion held no sway. Since he would not take the position, it was offered to one of the other three team members, and she took the "promotion."

Overnight, things changed among the four coworkers. The woman who took the new position was frequently summoned to closed-door meetings with the senior and executive pastor, and the other three had to answer directly to her. The team dynamic of mutual accountability and fellowship between the four was over. It lost its juice. It wasn't long until the remaining three team members resigned. The oppression, lack of trust and freedom, and the overall atmosphere of paternalism had become too much to bear.

## FAUX HEADSHIP

Paul refers to Jesus as the "head" several times in his letters to the churches.[8] Jesus' headship of the church is not debated theologically, and I've never once heard a pastor argue against it. Yet, despite this, we frequently hear the term "head pastor" used—not regarding Jesus but for a leader. I have often heard church members or pastors themselves refer to the pastor of a local church as "the head." This is more than an issue of bad semantics; it betrays theological box-checking, which is a tendency to say we believe one thing while practicing something different. When leadership is hierarchical, the headship of Jesus is thoroughly usurped by individuals acting as head of the family of Christ. It is a systemic issue. It is a structural issue. Hierarchical systems and structures in the body of Christ are a picture of subluxation. The spinal structure is in misalignment.

As we saw earlier in the book, our worldly leadership theories have led us to believe that people must be managed. This mindset produces hierarchies of chains of command. It is rooted in "it will not be so among you" worldly concepts of power and often nullifies the

---

8   See, for example, Eph 1:22, 4:15; Col 1:18, 2:10.

intelligence of Christ already present in the church. If we fall short in comprehending Jesus' ways and means, it will ensure a distorted leadership paradigm. We will lose the essence of the kingdom of God, which is so often counterintuitive to our natural way of thinking and operating. God's strength shines when our strength is brought to an end (2 Corinthians 12:9). The Lord's headship and strength are on display when we take an attitude and position of servile weakness. Injecting worldly power-plays into the kingdom is tantamount to introducing a cancerous agent into the body. And as brothers and sisters in Christ, we block the fruit and power of the Spirit when we create power structures over others. The fruit of spiritual leadership is nurtured in the powerless posture of servanthood.

Management systems may have been a great fit for early twentieth-century factories, but they are disastrous for families of adult siblings. As leaders in a church team, if we pause and reflect, we should question why, despite being gifted adults with the mind of Christ and living out the fruit of the Spirit, we are deemed insufficient to fulfill our calling without the help of management systems. Paul certainly believed the brothers and sisters in the church were adequate to the task,

> And concerning you, my brothers *and sisters*, I myself also am convinced that you yourselves are full of goodness, filled with all knowledge and able also to admonish one another.
>
> ROMANS 15:14 NASB

Paul was convinced that God's family was *filled* with goodness, know-how, and the ability to caution and exhort one another as the need arose. When we adopt worldly leadership structures and turn the church into a vendor of religious goods and services, we forfeit the church as a family, a key intention of the Lord all along. But when we realign to the headship of Jesus, his love flows down like a river, saturating the family of Christ with healing and maturing love that causes us to grow and be equipped for our calling. The church is not a corporation; it is a communal family, serving a benevolent and loving heavenly Father.

## For Teams to Process

- Do we regard our fellow leaders as "siblings" in Christ, respecting and valuing their input, rather than adhering strictly to a chain of command?
- How often do we seek the counsel of our fellow workers, rather than simply giving or receiving instructions?
- Are we creating an environment where every team member feels valued, heard, and trusted to carry out their responsibilities, or are we creating an atmosphere of command and control?
- Are we nurturing the growth of our members and creating a family-like environment, or are we falling into a corporate, transactional approach to church leadership?
- In what ways can we see that we are functioning as a family rather than a corporation?
- Do we see each other primarily as brothers and sisters in Christ, or as employees and coworkers?
- Is our communication open and honest (like a healthy family), or is it more formal and structured (like a business)?
- Is our primary focus on nurturing the spiritual growth of our members or on meeting organizational goals?
- How are decisions made within our team? Is it more of a top-down process (as in business), or is

it more collaborative and inclusive (as in a family setting)?

- Do we allocate time for fellowship, relationship-building, and shared experiences, or is our time together mainly focused on productivity and outcomes?
- How do we handle it when a staff member sins or fails in a major task? Does resolution happen in a loving, forgiving manner, or is it handled by more "senior" staff or HR?

# 6

# FELLOWSHIP OF EQUALS

## Realigning through Equality

*Leadership is not defined by the exercise of power but by the capacity to increase the sense of power among those led.*

MARY PARKER FOLLETT

*Jesus holds all authority. That means any little bit of power you and I have is derivative; we are dispatched under his authority. Jesus does not give authority to us; he retains it. Any power that you and I hold is God's and has been given to us by him for the sole purpose of glorifying him and blessing others.*

DIANE LANGBERG

One of my all-time favorite movies is the 1993 film *The Sandlot*.[1] It's worth watching for the soundtrack alone. Set in the summer of 1962, it tracks a group of talented baseball-obsessed boys, who need one more player to field a full team. Enter Scott Smalls, the new kid on the block who knows next to nothing about baseball. In fact, he is so bad that when his stepfather tries to teach him how to throw and catch, he ends up taking a ball to the face and gets a black eye. Encouraged by his

---

[1] *The Sandlot*, directed by David Mickey Evans (1993; Los Angeles, CA: 20th Century Fox).

mother, Smalls musters the courage to step onto the sacred sandlot, hoping to join the other boys on the team. But he quickly embarrasses himself with his lack of ability and acumen. He doesn't even know who "Babe" Ruth is—the Great Bambino!

The boys are adamant that Smalls doesn't have what it takes to be on the team. Every boy except Benny. The unelected leader and best player by far, Benny believes in the new kid and contends for the other boys to accept him. Amidst their criticisms of Smalls's inability, Benny points out the weaknesses in their own games, especially those protesting the loudest. "But you are part of the game, right?" he concludes. Refusing to take no for an answer, Benny begins to coach and encourage Smalls, who goes on to become a contributing member of the team, making plays in the outfield and hitting his first home run.

That is the power of *equipotency*. It is the power of unleashing everyone's potential in an atmosphere of equality. New York University professor and author Mila Baker writes:

> Organizational equipotency occurs in a coordinated networking system where everyone who works in the organization is working together *as equals*, toward a common goal. On any given day, I may assume different roles, yet I show up as an equal, regardless of the roles I play. I provide my assets to others, and I accept resources. I can help others. Although my position may enable or impede me from doing certain things at any given time, and work requirements may guide the role I assume, my personhood is always equal to everyone. Neither my role nor my position defines the degree of equality (or lack thereof) that I have as an individual in the organization—each individual serves as an equal and respected peer. I may not contribute the same way others do, but I make my contribution as an equal; I have the same opportunity to contribute, and the manner in which I contribute does not affect my standing in relation to another.[2]

---

[2] Mila Baker, *Peer-to-Peer Leadership: Why the Network Is the Leader* (Oakland, CA: Berrett-Koehler Publishers, 2014), 36–37.

## EQUALITY OF OPPORTUNITY

In a fellowship of equals, *equality of ability* is not the point. Most groups are made up of members with varying levels of skills, giftings, experience, and knowledge. But in a fellowship of equals, there is *equality of opportunity*, respect, and honor. Everyone carries equal status. If we don't get this right, we enter a place of distortion. We distort our own identities and the identities of others, and we cheapen and distort our own calling and the calling of God on others. These are weighty matters.

One of the chief marks of the way of the world—the way of the "Gentiles"—is seen in the pursuit of status. We see it in the chase for the latest in designer fashion, cars, and tech gadgets. This is why people will camp out at the Apple store to get the newest iPhone or watch, or rush to the sporting goods store to grab the newest Air Jordan sneakers. We are status-prone to the hilt. Sadly, this too often invades the church and feeds an unhealthy ambition that pulls us from the ways of Jesus and creates two types of people: those with an overly strong drive and those who lose all sense of aspiration. It inflates one person while it deflates the other. It puffs up one and takes the air out of another. When people are suppressed and over-managed, they tend to either become the ones at the top or shut down.

By failing to create a culture of equality, we unwittingly cultivate an atmosphere that encourages status-seeking. This sends us into the weeds and thickets of vainglory and off the pathway of the kingdom of God. Jesus warned his followers to not be like the scribes and Pharisees of his day, who lifted themselves above the everyday people:

"They love the place of honor at banquets, and the seats of honor in the synagogues, and personal greetings in the marketplaces, and being called Rabbi by the people. But as for you, do not be called Rabbi; for *only* One is your Teacher, and you are all brothers *and sisters*. And do not call *anyone* on earth your father; for *only* One is your Father, He who is in heaven. And do not be called leaders;

for *only* One is your Leader, *that is*, Christ. But the greatest of you shall be your servant. Whoever exalts himself shall be humbled, and whoever humbles himself shall be exalted. But woe to you, scribes and Pharisees, hypocrites, because you shut the kingdom of heaven in front of people; for you do not enter *it* yourselves, nor do you allow those who are entering to go in."

MATTHEW 23:6–13 NASB

## Swing and a Miss

When I was young and sporting a glorious business-in-the-front, party-in-the-back mullet, I was on staff with a team of two other pastors in a thriving Midwest church. The church was experiencing positive growth in virtually every sphere: mercy ministries, children, youth, young adults, discipleship, and weekend service participation. Above all, we were experiencing an incredible visitation of the Holy Spirit. It seemed almost every time we gathered for worship, there was a tangible anticipation that the Lord would touch us individually and corporately. And our expectations were not unmet. The breath of God blew in our midst, forging the deepest sense of community most of us had ever experienced. As a community of the Spirit grew, church members gathered spontaneously as often as they did at scheduled meeting times. Informal little groups gathered for morning coffee. Home groups met for discipleship and Bible study. Men's groups and women's groups regularly got away for retreats and times of refreshing in the Lord. New converts were emerging from almost every age group. Our church was more than a congregation; it had become an assembly of Jesus' followers.

The senior pastor was the epitome of an ideal shepherd. He was humble, had a heart of gold, and shared decision-making as well as almost everything involving strategic initiatives. He wanted each pastor to receive an equal salary and to teach and preach as often as they felt led. To this day, when I think of an archetypal pastor, I see his face. He had an incredible shepherd gifting. I remember one morning he came into the office late. It wasn't raining, yet he was soaking wet, with smudge marks on his forehead. "What in the world happened to you?" I asked. He was returning from fixing a toilet for an elderly couple in our church. Not surprising.

The other associate pastor was extremely gifted at administration and organization. He kept things on schedule and was great with details. His pulpit skills were not as strong as the senior pastor's or mine, but he had a solid enough teaching gift, and, on certain topics, he equipped the body well. My calling as a prophetic voice was developing, and there were seasons when I had a timely message or series the church needed to hear. Overall, I figure the senior pastor presented 65 percent of the sermons. For our church, this was a good balance. There was no tilt to one style of message, based on the gifting type of one individual. This kept our community on a stable footing.

If the senior pastor had presented most of the messages, our church would not have possessed the boundary-pushing perspective it had. His primary gift as a shepherd came out in almost every sermon—care and peaceful security—but not in a sappy and coddling way. It was solid and balanced. But he understood our members also needed to be challenged at times, and he often believed other voices on the team were better equipped to issue the challenge or recalibrate the message.

If I had been the sole preacher, it would not have been good. I would have been calling the men to wear kilts and war paint, and to be ready to fix bayonets at dawn to charge the enemy! If the other associate pastor had been the only speaker, we would have needed to double the strength of the coffee, just to keep our folks awake during yet another biblical genealogical list or lesson on Greek etymology as applied to the New Testament.

We were entering fields of ministry the church had never approached before. Through the various messages delivered via our diverse giftings, the body was nourished with encouragement, care, timely warning, and solid guidance for living as a discipling community. Our elders, who were not vocational staff members, also shared from time to time in our main services. They brought different perspectives from the ones we (the three paid leaders) brought. We were developing true shared leadership. And the body of Christ and our town was benefitting tremendously. The shared leadership culture allowed everyday Jesus-followers to experiment with their gifts and callings and saw the development of several outreaches and learning opportunities throughout our church and community.

We weren't using the latest church-growth models. They weren't necessary. We didn't need smoke machines and stage lighting as a substitute for the glory of the Lord. None of us had ever been part of a leadership team that was so serious about shared leadership. But frankly, we didn't know what we were doing or how to do it. And it eventually cost us. Foundational cracks were developing. Several church folks were in the ear of the senior pastor, saying he was supposed to be "number one" and, apart from when he was on vacation or a guest speaker was present, the church needed to hear from him. On the other hand, another group of people spoke glowingly when we, the other pastors, taught.

It is no wonder Satan sought a breach in the wall. The same thing happened in the early church, as even leading apostles split apart for a time in disagreement.[3] The enemy never stands by or gives up seeking to destroy the work of the Lord.

Eventually, the senior pastor's identity felt threatened, and paranoia crept in. On the one hand, he worried he was no longer needed, and the other associate pastor and I were pushing him out. On the other hand, he became anxious he was not fulfilling his obligation as *the Guy*. The credit for the growth was attributed to us as a team rather than solely to him, and without warning or conversation, he suddenly resigned. A short time later, he started another church nearby. It was crushing, and the fallout divided the church.

Within just a couple of years, this man realized his insecurities had gotten the best of him. He came to others and me in repentance, and I was eager to forgive and reconcile with him. We have enjoyed many

---

[3] See Acts 15:36–41, for example.

occasions of fellowship in the years that followed. Sadly, the damage had been done to the church, and there was no putting it back together.

## Making a Game Plan

That was three decades ago, and we cannot place the fault solely at the feet of the senior pastor. I know now that we *all* failed. Shared leadership doesn't automatically surface in the vacuum of hierarchy. We needed to develop a support system for it. At that time, the prevailing understanding of leadership was even more exclusively the default concept than it is today. It was naïve to think we could just operate as equals without proper systems and structures. And we further failed to grow the body of Christ in an understanding of leadership as servantship. Most of us had only ever seen or been part of churches with a primary solo-heroic leader.

We should have taught the church about the difference between top-down leadership and mutual leadership, and what we were seeking to accomplish. Were we on track in *practicing* shared leadership? Absolutely. But we continued with titles and organization charts that were top-down.

Most of the church folks were used to having *the Guy* as their leader. They expected to be led by some*one* at the top. And they cannot be fully blamed for this mindset. That was all they had ever known. It was altogether unwise, unreasonable, and unfair to expect the church to understand what we were trying to communicate and live out. You cannot operate in a "new" way without working on the structures and mindset of the body. If we had taken the time to teach New Testament servantship and develop structures and systems in that spirit, I am certain things would have turned out differently. New wine needs new wineskins.

A few short years back, I was visiting one of the most precious members of that church, Susan. She asked me why our sweet church fell apart. "What really happened?" she asked. I laid it all out, and she thanked me in tears for explaining the details. "It all makes sense now," she said. "I never knew that. Thank you so much for telling me this." I am convinced most of our church would have enthusiastically embraced the concept of shared leadership if they had been given a better understanding of what we were trying to do—and it would also have exponentially developed their own giftings and callings as servants of the Lord.

This cautionary tale offers many important lessons for leaders seeking a transition into a fellowship of equals. When a body has been paralyzed and is starting to walk again, rehabilitation is needed. It is vital to take small steps forward, and then rest. As dormant nerves and muscles begin to connect and fire, the body gets sore and needs to pace itself. We must do the necessary hard work of paradigm-shifting, which includes teaching the body how to mobilize itself, but not pushing it too hard, too fast. We must be patient.

## EQUALITY IN OUR WORDS

As I already mentioned, our pastoral staff embraced and practiced equality in leadership. However, we hadn't shifted the paradigms and developed the structures that would sustain and nurture the vision of shared leadership within our church. An essential aspect of conveying a new paradigm is through the titles and words we use.

### The Power of Titles

Jesus compels us to seek equality with one another and to run away from allowing or striving for top positions and titles. Psychologist and Catholic priest Eugene Kennedy writes,

> Jesus' words are not directed solely to a small band of zealots who corrupt Judaism, but to all religious leaders across the bands of time. Jesus speaks with such deep feeling because he wants his words to echo in all the courts and temples of history. He calls urgently, lovingly, to offer us friendship rather than domination,

a Kingdom of relationships rather than regulations, a kind of life in God that matches and does not contradict what is most richly human about us.[4]

Using graphic language, Jesus labels the religious leaders of the day as frauds and imposters who "shut the kingdom of heaven in people's faces" (Matthew 23:13). We often tend to view the Pharisees as religious fundamentalists who were obsessed with the law of Moses. But we seldom consider or realize Jesus' emphasis on their hypocrisy in setting themselves over their fellow brethren. They are Atlas imposters.

Jesus specifically forbids rank-based titles and practices that degrade the beauty of our sibling status under his rule. He says it is a blockade to the kingdom. The stakes are high. When we choose to ignore Jesus' warning, we prevent God's family from fully forming, discovering, and exercising their gifts and callings. Leadership in Jesus should always draw people into their kingdom destiny and identity. It should never do the opposite.

More often than I care to remember, I have brought up what Jesus said concerning rank-based titles to friends, colleagues, and in teaching settings, only to be met with silent stares, or—on more than one occasion—replies such as, "I couldn't really care less about titles one way or the other. They don't bother me." We really need to let this sink in. Such attitudes are tantamount to waving Jesus off. Jesus is emphatic about titles that elevate anyone above their kingdom siblings. Notice what Jesus is, in effect, saying in Matthew 23:6–10: "Don't allow yourself to be called _____. Don't call others _____. Don't call yourself _____." Could he be any clearer? He allows no place for titles that elevate and separate. It is not to be so among us. To disobey Jesus here slams the door to God's kingdom in the face of our brothers and sisters. Worse of all, it is slamming the door in Jesus'

---

4   Eugene Kennedy, *The Choice to Be Human: Jesus Alive in the Gospel of Matthew* (New York, NY: Doubleday, 1985), 212.

face. No wonder we find him standing at the door and knocking to get into his own church in the third chapter of Revelation.

Please hear me on this. Titles have their place in the church ... if they are the right titles. If they are not *status*-based. *Role*-based titles are useful; they help us focus on our primary tasks and help others connect with those at the frontlines of specific areas. But *rank*-based titles are different. They set a tone and affect the culture of any group. Up or down, in one direction or the other, they underscore status every time they are spoken or read. Such titles emphasize and highlight boundaries, privilege, and permission. Status titles create sociological and psychological dynamics of exclusivity and hierarchy.

Just think about the flicker that goes off in your mind when you meet someone new to you. Consider a scenario where you are introduced to two church pastors: "Meet Larry, senior pastor of First Church; and Sarah, associate pastor of First Church." If you are like most people, in a nanosecond your mind places different levels of status, and probably value, on Larry and Sarah. Furthermore, if you are a staff member of a church, depending on your own title, you most likely feel equal to, above, or lesser than Larry or Sarah. Unless you have the same rank-based title, equality goes out the door.

Speaking of titles, there is a strange dynamic concerning the title of "associate pastor." By definition, an associate means to be a partner or colleague. The word "colleague" comes from the conjunction of *co* and *league*—"to be in the same league." But that is not how we understand the word in our churches. Many of us think of an associate pastor as an assistant or junior guy or gal who is a rung or more below the senior and executive pastors. They don't yet have the chops or experience to ascend to senior status. But what is the witness of Scripture? In God's kingdom, we are *all* associates. Sometimes I wonder if it might be good for every pastor on the staff of a church to call themselves "associate pastor"! If we could garner the courage to change our terminology and titles, it would not only be a constant reminder to hold our own fleshly tendencies in check, but it would also provide opportunities to explain our core belief in our servantship and the headship of Christ, particularly when new folks ask, "Who is the senior pastor around here?"

Along with status-based titles, there are other telltale signs of whether a group or organization is indeed a fellowship of equals. Take a quick look at your church's website. On the staff page, check out the order of listing. Are team members listed alphabetically or based on rank? In virtually every church or faith-based organization, the listing is based on hierarchy—status and rank. I'm no statistician, but I just did a random internet search of ten churches. I looked at the websites of five large churches and five small- to mid-size churches. Bar none, every website listed the team in descending order of rank. If we honestly believe in equality, then we should perhaps consider listing our team members alphabetically.

## The Power of Words

As I've said before, language matters. It is not trivial. It shapes the direction of our conversations, cultivates paradigms, and forms our organizational cultures. Sometimes it is helpful to replace traditional biblical terms and language with terminology from vetted scholarly translations that make contemporary sense. I absolutely love reading Scripture in various versions to gain a better understanding and shake myself from preconceived notions of certain passages I have read hundreds of times. But when we substitute the words of Jesus and the epistles with vocabulary and titles that *conflict* with the aims and essence of our Lord's kingdom agenda, we go deep into the weeds of error on multiple levels.

Terminology can easily form strongholds in the mind that strangle the Spirit's work in our midst. Thoughtless and damaging language locks and blockades the doorways of creativity as well as openness to ways and means we previously had not considered. This even happens at times when an unbiased reading of the Scriptures should make the original meaning crystal clear. As Jesus said, "Thus you nullify the word of God by your tradition that you have handed down" (Mark 7:13 NIV).

For example, the New Testament term for those in local teams is never "staff" or "employee." The preferred word used in the letters to the churches is "coworker." It is translated into multiple forms: "fellow laborer," "helper," "fellow worker," "fellow helper," "workfellow," "companion," and more.[5] It is a beautiful term that evokes the power of Jesus' intent in pouring out various giftings. The Greek word is *synergasia*, from which we have the English word "synergy." The Lord gave us this beautiful variety of gifts to generate synergy among us! Here are but a few examples (emphases mine):

> Greet Priscilla and Aquila, my *co-workers* in Christ Jesus.
> ROMANS 16:3 NIV

> I have thought it necessary to send to you Epaphroditus my brother and *fellow worker* and fellow soldier, and your messenger and minister to my need.
> PHILIPPIANS 2:25

> [I] sent Timothy, our brother, and minister of God, and our *fellow laborer* in the gospel of Christ, to establish you, and comfort you concerning your faith.
> 1 THESSALONIANS 3:2 NKJV

Notice that Paul never said of those individuals, "They work for *me*." Regardless of your role at a church, there is not one person who works for *you*. They are your fellow workers, your companions, and fellow servants of the Lord. We all work for the Lord. They are not your staff. They are Jesus' staff.

My first opportunity to serve in a vocational role at a church was as a youth pastor. The senior pastor, Sam, was old enough to be my

---

[5]  Ford, et al., *The Starfish and the Spirit*, 126.

father. And during those years, I did some really dumb stuff. As I was thinking back on my time there, I literally face-palmed! True story. Though his wisdom, experience, and notoriety left me in the dust, Sam treated me as having an equal voice. Was I his equal in talent, experience, or giftings? Not by a long shot. I couldn't hold a candle to his ability to teach, counsel, lead others, or develop a church. I was not equal in those ways, but he *treated* me as an equal in the Lord.

I had the same Spirit of the Lord in me that Sam had. I had the same mind of Christ. And he treated me like an equal coworker. With Sam, I could share what I felt the Lord leading me to do in the youth ministry, and I was even free to share my thoughts on the direction of the whole church. This didn't mean Sam always acted on my opinion (and it's a good thing he didn't!), but he always considered my opinion and took it to heart. And the confidence that was instilled in me as I grew into my calling was immeasurable. This was the way Paul spoke of Timothy, his protégé. Though Timothy was a young man whose ability and stature paled in comparison, Paul referred to him on equal terms.

The sweet spot is all about the attitude, demeanor, and heart of the players involved. Though I had the same mind of Christ and the Holy Spirit as Sam, I did not have the same experience, nor was I directly responsible for the overall shepherding of the church. This is a prime example of the importance of being "persuaded" by another leader (which we covered in chapter four). Sam did not "despise [me] for [my] youth" (1 Timothy 4:12)—the very thing Paul instructed Timothy to refuse to accept. And I respected and valued Sam's wisdom as an elder. He gave genuine respect to my opinions, and I gave genuine respect to his broader responsibilities.

## EQUALITY IN THE BODY

In the story of my Midwest church's leadership fracture and fall, one of the main failures came from our church's bias toward having "leaders" and "followers." We all have a natural tendency to put some on pedestals and to exclude others from participating in displaying the fruit of church leadership.

## Misalignment of "Followers"

Alongside an escalation of leadership focus and language in recent years has been the idea of gaining *followers*. "How many Facebook followers do you have?" "So-and-so has half a million followers on her X account!"[6] "Why hasn't my Instagram account grown? I need more followers so I can have more influence!" The word "follower" has become a big deal. The accumulation of followers is not only a status symbol but can be a literal commodity. It is now possible to hire services that, for the right price, will get you more followers. The more worldwide web followers you have, the more valuable you are to sponsors or advertisers. In the realm of social media, followers are readers and listeners. They represent eyeballs watching for your next move and earlobes leaning in for your thoughts, opinions, and hot takes.

Among prevailing church leadership concepts, the importance of gaining followers takes on a similar but deeper meaning. It is hard to find literature or training content regarding leadership that is not spattered with the concept of gaining followers. One of the pithiest and most-frequently repeated statements leadership guru John Maxwell has made over the years is, "He who thinks he leads, but has no followers, is only taking a walk."[7] In front of a live audience, the declaration is always made with a wink and a nod—and the crowd inevitably chuckles. But the assertion is meant to be taken seriously and definitively. All leaders have followers, period. If you are going to be a leader, you must have followers. The subtitle of Maxwell's best-selling

---

6   X, formerly known as Twitter.

7   John C. Maxwell, *Maxwell Daily Reader: 365 Days of Insight to Develop the Leader Within You and Influence Those Around You* (Nashville, TN: Thomas Nelson, 2011), 9.

book, *The 21 Irrefutable Laws of Leadership*, is *Follow Them and People Will Follow You.*[8]

But are we really supposed to be garnering followers in our roles as servants in Jesus' church? Is the idea that we need to get people to follow *us*, in fact *irrefutable?*

For leaders in the church, the paradigm of gaining followers is a "supermeme," a term from author Jeffrey Nielson, who says,

> [A supermeme] is an unexamined belief, which is widely held by a society, or even by entire cultures. It governs how people see and think about reality, and so it determines how a people engage with others, community, and the world. Given their unexamined nature and that they are widely accepted as true, supermemes can cause a dysfunctional status quo to emerge, which may last for generations, if not millenniums. They are able to push out other ideas and block genuine reflection and thinking on better ways to live as human beings.[9]

The supermeme of gaining followers thrives on overtalk—where an idea is repeatedly mentioned as true without critical analysis until it becomes widely accepted without question. It is so immersed in our culture that it bypasses critique or deeper examination. The lexicon of our church culture often exposes our allegiance to individuals over allegiance to Jesus as Head of his church. It shows up in the everyday language of staff hierarchy.

Despite its contemporary emphasis and near absolute consensus among church leaders, the idea of getting people to follow us is not found in the New Testament. On the contrary, it is rebuked.

---

8  Maxwell, *The 21 Irrefutable Laws of Leadership.*

9  Jeffrey Nielson, "Deconstructing the Supermeme of Leadership: A Brief Invitation to Creating Peer-Based Communities & Leaderless Organizations," October 22, 2014, https://www.everywritersresource.com/selfpublished/deconstructing-supermeme-leadership/.

In the early days of the church, the elevation of God's servants had already begun:

> On the following day he entered Caesarea. Now Cornelius was expecting them and had called together his relatives and close friends. When Peter entered, Cornelius met him, and fell at his feet and worshiped *him*. But Peter helped him up, saying, "Stand up; I, too, am just a man."
>
> ACTS 10:24–26 NASB

In the Gospels, the concept of following Jesus is mentioned more than fifty times. Not once does Jesus tell his disciples to gather their own followers. The word "follower" is mentioned a mere seven times in the New Testament. Five times it refers to followers of Jesus and two times when Paul issues his Corinthian rebuke. As we move to the epistles, we are instructed many times about following, but apart from following Jesus, there is not one *who* to follow. We are only instructed as to *what* to follow:

Follow:

- things that make peace and edify one another (Romans 14:19)
- charity (1 Corinthians 14:1)
- that which is good (1 Thessalonians 5:15)
- righteousness, godliness, faith, love, patience, meekness (1 Timothy 6:11)
- righteousness, faith, love, and peace (2 Timothy 2:22)
- peace and holiness (Hebrews 12:14)
- faith (Hebrews 13:7)
- the suffering of Jesus (1 Peter 2:21)
- that which is good (3 John 1:11)

Several times Paul says, "imitate me," but that instruction is better translated as "imitate my ways"—which are not actually his ways but Christ's. He is calling people to imitate him as he imitates Christ. The concept of following as imitation is entirely different from following an individual intrinsically.

The early church exhibited a pattern of immaturity and continual conflict in several areas, which is one of the reasons why Paul wrote letters to them. The church at Corinth, for example, was elevating and following mere men, to the point of schism. In effect, they were creating the first batch of Christian celebrities. But, unlike so many instances we have witnessed in recent years, the men (servants of Jesus) refused to be put on pedestals. Of all the messy issues in the Corinthian church he had to deal with, Paul deals first with the issue of following men rather than following Christ. It was that important.

In the second verse of 1 Corinthians, Paul makes it clear that the words he is about to write are meant for the universal church.

> To the church of God that is in Corinth, to those sanctified in Christ Jesus, called to be saints together with all those who in every place call upon the name of our Lord Jesus Christ, both their Lord and ours.
>
> 1 CORINTHIANS 1:2

Notice that Paul doesn't write to the church of Corinth; he writes to the "church of God that is in Corinth." He is reminding these Christians that they are God's church. Their faith community happens to be in Corinth, but that is not their identity. Their distinctiveness is derived from being the Lord's people.

He writes to all those who are "sanctified," an old term that today sounds a bit religious but is packed with deep meaning. The root of the word is the idea of *separation*. The Greek word does not mean to separate in terms of a different location or a withdrawal from others; it means to be "set apart" or dedicated by the owner for a specific purpose. There is to be a difference in those who are sanctified. Furthermore, Paul uses the term "saints" for those (us included) who follow Jesus. We don't need a hierarchy from Rome to declare who is or is not a saint. The Holy Spirit has already done so. "All those who in every place call upon the name of our Lord Jesus Christ" are saints.

Paul, under the influence of the Holy Spirit, crafted these opening words purposefully. He has set the nail with an initial tap and is about to give a second intentional tap before driving home a major point. The point? This entire operation—everything about the church—is by, for, and unto God's glory. It is not built by an individual mortal. Humans can place no claim on it. And humans are never to receive glory for what happens in the church of the Lord Jesus Christ. *God* has equipped the church—which is the people—with everything needed to get the job done.

> I give thanks to God always for you because of the grace of God which was given you in Christ Jesus, that in every way you were enriched in him with all speech and all knowledge—even as the testimony to Christ was confirmed among you—so that you are not lacking in any spiritual gift, as you wait for the revealing of our Lord Jesus Christ.
>
> 1 CORINTHIANS 1:4–7 RSV

Remember, this letter is written to the church. It is intended to be read to the gathered people. It is not a letter to individual Christians. The context is plurality. What Paul is saying is true about the assembled, joined-together, people of God. There is nothing missing from the church as God's people. Every necessary spiritual gift has been poured out by the grace of God upon the ordinary collective of saints. As we explored in chapter three, the Greek word for "gift" in the passage above is *charisma*—divine empowerment or a grace gift. This is the same word used in 1 Corinthians 12 when Paul lists what we commonly call "spiritual gifts," as well as several other passages.[10]

Next, Paul gets to the brass tacks of bringing correction to the first of several problems within the Corinthian church.

> I appeal to you, brothers and sisters, in the name of our Lord Jesus Christ, that all of you agree with one another in what you say and

---

[10] See Rom 12:6; 1 Cor 7:7, 12:4, 9, 28, 30–31; 1 Tim 4:14; 2 Tim 1:6; 1 Pet 4:10.

that there be no divisions among you, but that you be perfectly united in mind and thought. My brothers and sisters, some from Chloe's household have informed me that there are quarrels among you. What I mean is this: One of you says, "I follow Paul"; another, "I follow Apollos"; another, "I follow Cephas"; still another, "I follow Christ."

Is Christ divided? Was Paul crucified for you? Were you baptized in the name of Paul?

1 CORINTHIANS 1:10-13 NIV

Paul has it on good authority that the saints in the church have lifted up particular servants of Jesus to the point of calling themselves their followers. Clearly, a degree of uppityness and pride has gone to seed as they take the side of their chosen celebrity leader. "I go to Joe Coolpastor's church." "Well, I am a follower of Sam Superpreacher's ministry," and so forth. This division is breaking Paul's heart, and he is appealing to their sensibilities. Twice he addresses them as "brothers and sisters." This is not only intended to soften the tone of his rebuke but to also remind them that he himself—one of the subjects of the followership schism—is nothing but their spiritual sibling.

A key term is used in the text, which speaks to realigning the vertebrae of the body of Christ to its true Atlas. New Testament scholar William Barclay comments, "[Paul] wishes them to be *knit together* (united), a medical word used of knitting together bones that have been fractured or joining together a joint that has been dislocated. The disunion is unnatural and must be cured for the sake of the health and efficiency of the body of the Church."[11] Paul is trying to get the church to realign the vertebrae of Christ's body to the headship of Christ.

---

[11] William Barclay, *The Daily Study Bible Series: The Letters to the Corinthians* (Philadelphia, PA: Westminster John Knox Press, 1975), 14.

## The Other Half

For churches to function as healthy bodies, we must fervently and intentionally seek to embrace equality. This includes equality of women as well. The intelligence of the body of Christ includes many wisdom-filled and gifted sisters in the Lord. To eliminate women from leadership is literally to sideline at least half of the team and to cut off unique aspects, insights, strengths, and skills that only the female side of humanity can offer. Just imagine a football team taking the field with only five or six players. Or a baseball team trotting out with only five fielders. It is an exercise in foolishness and futility.

It should be counted as redundant at this point in the history of theological scholarship to find it necessary to make a case for women in leadership. Unfortunately, we still must do so. For me, it is tantamount to making the case that the earth is round. The only argument we *should* have to make is a resounding "Duh!" Thankfully, in recent years, many theologians have provided solid scholarship on the theological affirmation for women to bear the fruit of leadership.

In addition to the women throughout the Old Testament (such as Ruth, Esther, and Deborah) who were used by the Lord to accomplish his purposes, the witness of the New Testament presents several examples of women participating in leadership and the shaping of the church.

In Romans 16, Paul mentions the following women by name:

- Phoebe—Paul describes her as a "servant of the church at Cenchreae" and asks the believers in Rome to welcome her in a way worthy of the saints (v. 1).
- Prisca (also known as Priscilla)—Paul mentions her along with her husband, Aquila, saying that they "risked their necks" for him (v. 3).
- Mary—Paul refers to her as one of the people who "worked hard for you" (v. 6).

- Junia—Paul describes her and her husband, Andronicus, as "prominent among the apostles" and "outstanding in the view of the apostles" (v. 7 NASB).
- Tryphena and Tryphosa—Paul calls these women "workers in the Lord" (v. 12).
- Persis—Paul acknowledges her as one of the people who "has worked hard in the Lord" (v. 12).
- Rufus' mother—Paul mentions her as someone who "has been a mother to me" and asks the believers in Rome to give her his greetings (v. 13).

For those who maintain that women are barred from senior leadership positions in the church, I would first highlight the case made by this entire book—the New Testament provides no place for "senior" positions for men either. Second, to make such a stance based on one or two passages from the epistles is both myopic and lacks the epistemological discipline of holding the entire New Testament text in context. On the role of women in the New Testament, theological professor Howard Snyder writes:

How we understand Scripture is, of course, the crucial question here. In the first place, we should start with "all that Jesus began to do and to teach" (Acts 1:1) before rushing on to Paul and the other New Testament writers. We should note, for example, Jesus' respect for women, his twelve or more woman disciples, and the marked prominence of women in Luke and Acts. According to Luke, women accompanied Jesus as he "traveled about from one town and village to another, proclaiming the good news of the kingdom of God" (Luke 8:1–13). Was not Jesus demonstrating something about the good news of the Kingdom by taking women with him on these tours? Second, we need to be careful in the way we interpret biblical truths. The Bible gives us clear, basic, shaping truths. The more obscure or troublesome biblical passages must be interpreted so that they do not cancel out or compromise these basic truths. For example, the teaching to be subject to political authority should not be interpreted so that it compromises our allegiance to Jesus Christ. Concerning women, this means that none of Paul's statements must be interpreted in such a way that they undercut fundamental truths, such as Galatians 3:28—in the church "there is neither Jew nor Greek, slave nor free, male nor female, for you are all on in Christ Jesus."[12]

On a personal level, I can't imagine my own journey of being shaped as a disciple apart from the influence and input of many women: Margie Spence, Debra Hirsch, Linda Bergquist, Brenda Salter McNeil, MaryKate Morse, Mindy Caliguire, Tammy Dunahoo, Jo Saxton, Freda Lindsay, Margaret Wheatley ... on and on.

## The Beauty of Ethnicity

As a white man—now an old white man—it has become increasingly clear to me that my bias of seeing through the lenses of my race has caused me to miss out on a deeper journey with the Lord. I know this is true for countless others as well. The beauty of the diverse perspectives of men and women of color is not only a gift the Lord gives to the entire world, but is also, and more particularly, God's certain plan and intention. Our world is a multiethnic amalgamation that God created to shape every human into his ultimate image. For us to grow in understanding God's will and ways, we must all know and grow in relationship and understanding with those who come from different backgrounds and perspectives than ourselves, including those of different ethnicities.

One of the leading lights in helping the church gain a better understanding and plan for ethnic equality is Mark DeYmaz and his Mosaix initiatives. Their website (mosaix.info) advocates for developing purposeful multiethnic churches:

---

[12]  Howard Snyder, *Liberating the Church: The Ecology of Church and Kingdom* (Westmont, IL: InterVarsity Press, 1983), 225–226.

A healthy multiethnic church is one in which people of diverse ethnic and economic backgrounds will themselves to:

- Walk, work, and worship God together as one to advance a credible witness of God's love for all people.
- Recognize, renew, reconcile, and redeem broken relationships, both interpersonal and collective.
- Establish equitable systems of responsible authority, leadership, governance, and accountability within the congregation.
- Advocate and advance justice, mercy, and compassionate work in the community.
- Embrace the tension of sound theological reflection and applicational relevance in an increasingly complex and intersectional society for the sake of the Gospel.[13]

Mosaix offers a cultural intelligence assessment and training for churches and faith-based organizations.

## EQUALITY IN POWER

The familiar adage "information is power" is a fair statement. And if we are serious about laying down our own power in order for the power of the Lord to prevail in all things, including our churches and systems of leadership, then information should be accessible to all as much as possible. If power is to be shared, information should be shared.

### Out of the Darkness and Into the Light

Years after the fall of our Midwest church, most church members had no idea what really happened or why. We had failed to create transparency in our body. Whether it was to protect ourselves or the rest of the church members, information was withheld, and fractures

---

[13] https://mosaix.info/healthy-multi-ethnic-church/.

were created. To combat power imbalances, we must have a culture of transparency.

One of my favorite burger joints started in the Midwestern United States. I must admit it's way too easy to get about three days' worth of calories in one meal with a steak burger, an order of cheese fries, and a cherry-on-top chocolate milkshake at this place. Steak 'n Shake began in the 1930s, with a promise of quality ground-beef burgers. The founder, Gus Belt, would roll in a barrel of T-bone, sirloin, and round steaks and grind them into a blend of ground beef right in the middle of his restaurant for everyone to see. Because refrigerators were rare at the time, eating spoiled meats was a legitimate public concern. Ground beef was often a mix of out-of-date meats, and therefore patrons rarely knew what food had been blended into the concoction they ate. But Belt chose to be transparent and allow his clientele to see what they were getting. He coined the phrase, "In Sight It Must Be Right," which he used as a tagline, emphasizing his confidence in serving fresh, quality ground beef.

Transparency is a hallmark of the kingdom of heaven. In fact, the idea of God as *light* runs throughout the Scriptures and is strongly emphasized in the New Testament.

God's very nature is light:

For at one time you were darkness, but now you are light in the Lord. Walk as children of light (for the fruit of light is found in all that is good and right and true).
EPHESIANS 5:8–9

But you are a chosen race, a royal priesthood, a holy nation, a people for his own possession, that you may proclaim the excellencies of him who called you out of darkness into his marvelous light.
1 PETER 2:9

In him was life, and the life was the light of men. The light shines in the darkness, and the darkness has not overcome it.
JOHN 1:4–5

If we walk in the light, as he is in the light, we have fellowship with one another, and the blood of Jesus his Son cleanses us from all sin.

1 JOHN 1:7

And this is the judgment: the light has come into the world, and people loved the darkness rather than the light because their works were evil. For everyone who does wicked things hates the light and does not come to the light, lest his works should be exposed. But whoever does what is true comes to the light, so that it may be clearly seen that his works have been carried out in God.

JOHN 3:19–21

Controlling cultures have a lot of shadows and darkness about them. They include plenty of closed-door meetings and redacted information. In churches that operate this way, not only are "lower-level" staff members left in the dark on matters that should be shared more broadly, but the congregation is as well. Church members only see the public persona of "upper-level" leaders. From what they can see, under the Sunday morning spotlights, Pastor Bill is a great guy. But staff members know better. They are just too afraid and controlled to expose the guy who signs their checks.

## Controlling Conversations

In the human body, every cell receives a free flow of information. This is the key to life in the body. It is the key to growth. When information is blocked, *formation* is blocked. And paralysis or death is sure to follow.

I know of too many accounts of leadership cultures in churches whereby top-level leaders—usually called the "executive team"—hold back information from "lower-level" staff. Information is privileged. If you are not one of the privileged ones, you don't get access to all the information.

This does not mean that all matters should be published openly. Confidentiality is vital in personal matters, such as information that surfaces in counseling or personal crises of individuals. This is different from *privileged* information, which people guard to shield themselves for their own benefit.

And can you fathom Jesus demanding that one of his disciples sign a non-disclosure agreement? The idea is laughable. To even try to imagine the scene of Jesus sitting behind a desk and pushing the paperwork across the table is a headshaking scenario. Jesus hands you a pen and says, "Sign this if you want your severance." Yet this has become common practice in churches across the US. I've heard of too many church staff members who were forced out of their jobs and compelled to sign an NDA to receive their justly deserved severance. Clearly, the ones in power were aware that the facts of the situation would not sit well with others—including church members—if the truth was brought into the light. Practices such as this come from cultures of darkness. For cultures of Christ, employing such practices should be considered a preschool-level no-no. They lock and unlock doorways and information portals and place limits on openness and authenticity. The spirit of darkness is behind them.

The human body is a free-flowing, no-holds-barred network of information. Our life depends upon it operating this way. It is unthinkable to imagine certain organs or cells in our bodies holding back information from other organs, limbs, or nodes. This is another reason we must first think *biology* rather than *business* when it comes to leadership cultures in our churches. Can you imagine our legs making plans to take the rest of the body into a lake or swamp without thinking it through with the rest of the body? The brain, lungs, nose, and mouth at least would certainly need to be consulted.

Conversations are often controlled in domineering leadership cultures by appealing to the notion that the senior pastor is not to be questioned—they are to be obeyed. To push back on a proposal or directive is forbidden. As a staff member, I have experienced this, and it is one of the most common issues raised by staff members serving under command-and-control leaders. The fragility of egoism and narcissism in so many senior leaders allows no place for discussion. Not only is this a "not so among you" issue, but it also cuts off the intelligence and wisdom of the body. Most often, however, the policy of not questioning the senior leader is not official—it is an unwritten bully street code in the staff's culture.

Any leadership culture that lets senior pastors or executive-level leaders get by with patterns of habitually not showing the fruit of the Spirit, while holding "lower-ranking" staff members to stricter standards, is guilty of the sin of showing partiality.

> Do not accept an accusation against an elder except on the basis of two or three witnesses. Those who continue in sin, rebuke in the presence of all, so that the rest also will be fearful *of sinning*. I solemnly exhort you in the presence of God and of Christ Jesus and of *His* chosen angels, to maintain these *principles* without bias, doing nothing in a *spirit of* partiality.
>
> 1 TIMOTHY 5:19–21 NASB

For our churches and faith-based organizations to function as healthy bodies, we must embrace equality.

Interrogations can also be a form of controlling conversation. Have you ever been told, "Meet me in my office," and when you showed up, there was a third person or more already there? This is a typical tactic of domination. The executive leaders call a "lower-level" leader in, not for a conversation, but for an interrogation—and the setting, with its aura of threat, is designed to intimidate and overwhelm. "Did you tell so-and-so such-and-such?" "We have heard that you have been ... Is this true?" Such ways and means are neither from the kingdom of heaven nor the Holy Spirit.

> Brothers *and sisters*, even if a person is caught in any wrongdoing, you who are spiritual are to restore such a person in a spirit of gentleness.
>
> GALATIANS 6:1 NASB

Take note—"*even if.*" Even if the person is guilty of wrongdoing, a spirit of gentleness is to prevail. Leaders who practice the habits we've been discussing are unfit for leading. But these and other tactics of intimidation are quite common in many churches of our day.

## Church Competition

The idea that some churches require staff members to sign non-compete agreements is so far out there that if you have never heard of such a thing, you probably have a hard time believing it takes place. It does. There are indeed pastors who view themselves as "owning" a territory. Not unlike an NDA, to receive severance, or as a requirement at the beginning of employment, the individual is required to sign an agreement to not serve at another church or start another church within a particular-mile radius of the employing church. Think this one through. First off, consider the word *compete*. Who is the competition between? If Jesus has planted the employing church—if it is indeed *his* church—is Jesus worried about someone competing with him? The only way a competition could even take place is if there was a competition between humans, flesh vs. flesh. If a senior pastor wants a non-compete agreement, he or she has just exposed something that is beyond shameful. His or her heart has gotten far from the Holy Spirit and instead is full of ambition to build his or her own kingdom and not Christ's.

Instead of competition, we need to strive for collaboration. We need to use our gifts, powers, and privileges to lift others up, not just ourselves. But because we have spent so long jockeying for position, we don't know what collaboration looks like, and instead we resort to competition.

An example comes from something my mother once said to me after I gave her a copy of my first published book—*Right Here, Right Now*—which was coauthored with Alan Hirsch.[14] Over the last couple

---

[14]  Alan Hirsch and Lance Ford, *Right Here, Right Now: Everyday Mission for Everyday People* (Grand Rapids, MI: Baker Books, 2011).

of decades, Alan has had an immeasurable impact and influence on the evangelical church. His insights and writing have shaped the church in historic ways. Fortunately for me, Alan became a friend and mentor a long time ago, and I wrangled him into writing a book with me. Not that I care to or claim to be well known today, but at the time I was mostly unknown! A week after I gave my elderly mom a copy of that first book, she told me she thought it was wonderful, but there was just one thing she would prefer. "I just wish that other fella's name wasn't on it," she said. I couldn't help myself from chuckling as I responded, "Momma, I know you don't know who Alan is, but trust me. If his name wasn't on the book, my name wouldn't be on it either—because it would not have been published."

One evening many years ago, Alan and I were in Texas for a conference. We had a meal with a group of leaders from a church that was gaining popularity. I knew a couple of the guys around the table but had not met most of them. I was seated directly across from the senior pastor of this church, and at some point in the evening, I asked him a question. I don't even remember what it was. But he was looking straight at me when I asked it. His response was peculiar. He just stared at me with no expression. It wasn't especially loud in the room, but I thought maybe he hadn't heard me, although he had to at least have seen my lips moving. I was looking straight at him. So I asked the question again. Still no response. He just looked at me blankly and then turned away. *Well, that was weird,* I thought to myself. *I'm pretty sure I just got dissed by this young, rising-up-the-celebrity-leadership-ladder pastor.* As our time together came to a close, our waitress came to the table with the bill. The senior pastor told her to put his meal, Alan's meal, and his staff's meal on his tab. He pointed at me and said, "That guy's on his own." Wow, dissed again! It was clear I was a nobody in his eyes. I was not worthy to be conversed with, much less to be bought a meal.

Later in the evening, Alan and I, along with our friend, author Neil Cole, were in the lounge area of our hotel. At one point, Alan went to grab a drink, and a lone, young man was ordering a drink as well. I noticed the two of them chatting. A few minutes later, Alan had rejoined us, and the young man received his drink and went to sit down at a table. "Brother!" Alan motioned, "Come join us!" Alan introduced the young man to Neil and me, "Guys, this is Barkley. I just met him. He's from Boise and is here at the conference by himself." What a difference between the two scenarios that evening.

As I lay in my bed that night, I remembered an evening several years earlier, and thought about how I was able to coauthor a book with Alan. Many years ago, I was in Pasadena, sitting alone in a restaurant full of people I didn't know. I had never met Alan previously, but he came over, sat next to me, and we talked over the next couple of hours. From the first evening to today, we have collaborated on two books, developed myriad training pieces, joined with others to start networks, and have had tons of fun. But what I know is that I am not a special case. Alan has done the same with many others. Humility is the foundation of the mindset that develops a culture of equality. Alan is sober in his measure of faith in his giftings. The payoff is a Holy Spirit synergy that the gift-mix Jesus pours out on individuals yields for the sake of the whole.

I know that even though we have many of the same giftings, Alan's "measure of faith" in those gifts is greater than mine. But when we are working together, this has never held me back. This is because of Alan's character, maturity, and sobriety. In the words of Paul, he is not thinking "of himself more highly than he ought to think" (Romans 12:3). He treats others as equals. This allows the measure of faith in our gifts to empower us when we feel compelled to share an idea or insight on a project we are working on together. We can function together with confidence and not by holding or shrinking back.

Over the years, I have witnessed Alan defer to and encourage younger or less-experienced men and women to step up with their giftings more times than I can count. And I have watched those younger folks soar and flourish into powerful contributors to the mission of Jesus. The payoff comes as the gifts Jesus has poured out are manifested and mutually benefit everyone. The body of Christ grows, experiences greater health, and functions properly.

## The Second-Chair Error

One of the most dangerous errors in recent church leadership cultures is creation of *the second chair*. This is the position or office that often operates under the title of "executive pastor." I've recently heard that some advocates call it "secondary leadership." Not only is this idea erroneous, but it also devastates the giftings of others and feeds the narcissistic domineering power base of the "not so among you" cultures in many churches. By definition, when we hear the word "secondary," we tend to think of something that comes after, is less important than, or is a result of that which is primary. No precedent can be found for such a concept, much less prescription, of first- and second-chair leadership in Jesus' church. There is no "second chair" because there is no "first chair" in the church Jesus builds.

In the corporate business world, decisions are made at the top and flow downward. Policy, programming, scheduling, and products are decided upon, and orders are sent down the ladder for execution. And in many churches, this is also normative:

- "Pastor Joey wants us to do five Christmas Eve services, so everyone has to be there."
- "We are going to begin a downtown outreach. Make it happen."
- "Here are the new office hours that have been decided upon."
- "From this point forward, all department leaders must fill out the following weekly report and turn it in to the executive pastor."

Most church leaders will read these statements and consider them normal. But the kingdom of God is not *normative*. It is abnormal to the typical mind. The church is not the business world, and church staff members are not to be treated as troops to be handed marching orders. I realize this concept is a mindblower for those who are used to bossing others and being bossed by "higher-ups." Remember, you must learn to trust your team members. The ones you are *among*.

Typically, it is a small nucleus of executive team members who tell others what to do and when to do it—but the ethos of the kingdom of heaven in Jesus' church is the great leveler. When we allow ourselves and others to operate apart from the form and function of this beautiful equality, we become imbalanced and eventually teeter on the brink of disaster. When we operate in the joyful culture of equality in Christ, we can begin to experience all the Lord offers us.

## For Teams to Process

- How do we currently make decisions within the team? Are all team members encouraged to contribute their ideas and perspectives, or do certain individuals dominate decision-making?
- Do we have a culture of transparency within the team? Are information and communication flowing freely, or are certain team members kept in the dark about important matters?
- Are there any unwritten rules or norms within the team that promote hierarchy or favor certain team members over others? How can we challenge and change those norms to foster a more equal and inclusive environment?
- How do we handle disagreements and conflicts within the team? Are all team members encouraged to express their opinions and concerns, or is questioning the leadership discouraged?
- How are team members recognized and appreciated for their contributions? Is there a tendency to elevate certain individuals as celebrities or to create a hierarchy based on perceived importance?

- How can we shift our language and terminology to reflect a culture of equality and mutual respect? Are there any rank- or status-based titles or terms we should reconsider?
- Do we actively promote diversity and inclusion within the team? How can we ensure that all voices, including those from different ethnic backgrounds and genders, are heard and valued?
- What steps can we take to ensure that everyone on the team has equal access to opportunities for growth, development, and advancement?
- Are there any power imbalances within the team? How can we address these imbalances and ensure that power is shared and distributed equitably?
- How can we foster a culture where questioning and challenging ideas are seen as constructive and valuable practices rather than threats to authority?
- How can we encourage mutual support and cooperation within the team, so that everyone feels valued and empowered to contribute their unique gifts and talents?
- What concrete actions can we take to promote a culture of equality, transparency, and mutual leadership within our team and organization?

# 7

# UNTAPPED WISDOM

## Realigning With the Wisdom of the Older Ones

*Wisdom is with the aged,*
And with *long life* comes *understanding.*

JOB 12:12 NASB

*And your ancient ruins shall be rebuilt; you shall raise up*
*the foundations of many generations; you shall be called the*
*repairer of the breach, the restorer of streets to dwell in.*

ISAIAH 58:12

In 1961, an enigma in the small Pennsylvanian borough of Roseto caught the eye of the medical profession. The conundrum involved pasta, wine, smoking, soot ... and heart health. It came to the attention of a local heart specialist that, unlike the surrounding communities, the Rosetans had an unusually low rate of heart disease. In fact, in this little township, originating from a settlement of Italian immigrants, the rate of heart attacks in men under sixty-five was half the national average.[1] Researchers sought the answer to why the residents had

---

[1] Marshall Chang, "The Roseto Effect—A lesson on the true cause of heart disease," *Unimed Living*, https://www.unimedliving.com/living-medicine/illness-and-disease/the-roseto-effect-a-lesson-on-the-true-cause-of-heart-disease.html.

such good heart health. Surely it was linked to their diet and healthy lifestyle!

But the investigators quickly discovered the folks lived on a steady diet of high-cholesterol Italian foods, drank more than their fair share of wine, and smoked crazy amounts of cigarettes. And to top it all off, the main industry was slate mining, which coated the men's naval cavities and lungs with sludge and dust. The answer had to lie elsewhere.

So anthropologists descended upon the little town to get to the bottom of things. Along the way, they discovered more astounding facts about Roseto. The crime rate was zero. None. Nada. And no one was enrolled in governmental assistance programs. Great heart health, no crime, and even the poorest among them had their needs met.

Through a series of studies initiated by the University of Oklahoma, researchers proposed that the best explanation for the longevity of Rosetans was their close-knit family ties and strong community cohesion. Not only did the little migrant settlement have good physical hearts, but they also had good emotional hearts. The "Roseto Effect" became well known, and in the ensuing years, several articles, papers, and accounts have been published on the phenomenon.

Among the many contributing factors to the Roseto Effect, one of the things researchers highlighted was the community's perspective on its older citizens. Researchers discovered that most households had three generations living under one roof. But they also uncovered another significant factor: The town had established an unofficial council of the elderly, to which residents could bring everything from marriage conflicts to disputes between neighbors. It was found that the wisdom and advice of the older folks could often help to mediate and bring relational solutions to those who were at odds with one another or were struggling with other issues.

Roseto had not pushed older people to the side. Far from it. They had drawn them to the center. They valued and esteemed the experience of the aunts and uncles, the grandmas and grandpas. The elders among them were viewed as a gift to the community. Why did Roseto have better hearts than those living close by? At least in part, it was because they were tapping into the hearts of the senior generation.[2]

In modern Western culture, we have largely lost our capacity to understand what a treasure we have in the older people in our midst. Sure, we have the right terms for them—*senior citizens.* They are our seniors, and they are citizens. But we have lost the expectation that they have much to offer in helping our citizenry to live better lives.

## A MULTIGENERATIONAL CHURCH PROBLEM

Along these lines, something concerning has caught my attention over the years with young or recently planted churches in North America. When I meet with a new church's leadership team and elders, or scan the "elders" listed on church websites, too often they are not actually *elders*. At most, they are the eld*est*. Often, it's a group of young people who very well may be the most mature and seasoned among a church of predominantly young singles and newly married couples. So, they may indeed be the *eldest*, but they are not *older ones* in the biblical sense.

Don't hear me wrong. Church leadership takes a lot of energy. There is no getting around time-sensitive, logistical, and operational necessities—all of which require a lot of drive. We often need the horsepower and insight of younger people. There are also cultural factors that come into play. A church in a setting of young singles and couples needs to be relatable. Young, gifted men and women who lead well are more likely to gain the attention of their sociological peers. Life works like that. Trends in architecture, music, technology, and the like are constantly changing. It takes the sensibilities of youthfulness to get at what matters in those areas. And it requires stamina to keep up with the changes—something that lessens with age.

---

[2]  See Rafid Hossain, "The Roseto Effect: The secret to a long life," *The Business Standard*, October 13, 2022, https://www.tbsnews.net/thoughts/roseto-effect-secret-long-life-512826#.

As I write this, I am one birthday candle away from sixty. And yes, it feels like just yesterday that I was a thirty-year-old church planter. I am in decent shape for my age and can hold my own in conversations with the young people and pastors I work with. I'm not out of touch … for the most part. I can say the same about many of my friends and colleagues in my age bracket. But there is no getting around it: We are in a different stage of life. The issues that concern us and the things we give our attention to are different from those that preoccupy a thirty-something pastor or church planter. And that is a good thing—on both counts.

What color scheme should the church website go with? We old guys couldn't care less. Twenty years ago, we would think about it and debate it for hours, if not days. Now? Go with pink and purple as far as we're concerned! Just don't mess up the coffee. Thank the Lord the younger ones think about the details. They have the eye to see them and the energy to look after them. We geezers, not so much. We are thinking about other things—like where we left our reading glasses. Different generations think differently. But it goes much further, much deeper.

We need each generation to do what their generation does best. And we need each generation to speak to, listen to, and learn from both the previous and upcoming generations. Deeper still, we need to live this way. We need regular connection and fellowship among generations to sharpen and soften one another as needed. The younger ones need the elders, and the elders need the younger ones. We need the foundation of multiple generations.

The evangelical church has not always done a good job at this. In fact, we have unwittingly encouraged the separation of generations. We divide them into children's ministry, youth ministry, young adults, young singles, college and career, senior groups, and so forth. Though it can be helpful for individuals to meet in their own age category, when we overdo such divisions, we lose the collective strength and intelligence of the body.

This runs both ways. Think about it. If you are in your forties or older and are having trouble navigating an app or finding something on your phone or device, who do you turn to for help? Probably a twelve-year-old, or younger! If you need to understand what some new term is, you may turn to a twenty-something to explain it to you. You feel so cool and enlightened that you no longer think TikTok must be the newest Apple watch.

Our lives move forward in seasons and phases. We have ups and downs, wins and losses, disappointments, and dreams fulfilled. Through it all, we are learning lessons and retaking the tests we fail. The most affordable education is learning from someone who has already paid for theirs. As we progress through the phases of our lives, we need the help of those who have been down those trails already.

## REDISCOVERING WISE ELDERS

Former Fuller Seminary Professor of Leadership J. Robert ("Bobby") Clinton has influenced thousands of leaders, young and old. His work, which he termed "Leadership Emergence Theory," has been instrumental in helping many understand and navigate the seasons, transitions, and outcomes along the timeline of a leader's life.[3] Don't let the term "leader" sidetrack you. Clinton is the first to advocate for the priesthood of all believers and that leadership in the kingdom of God is not limited to "vocational" ministers. This is for all of us.

Like so many others, I was blessed to be a student of Bobby Clinton before he retired. His insight helped me in my late thirties, throughout my forties, and today as I close out my fifties. Clinton studied thousands of leaders throughout history and concluded that there are generally five phases of a leader's life, along with transitions from phase to phase.[4] Clearly, there are exceptions, but time and again this timeline coincides with many people's lifelong development.

---

[3] Dr. J. Robert Clinton, *Leadership Emergence Patterns: A Self-Study Manual for Evaluating Leadership Selection Processes* (Barnabas Resources, 1984).

[4] In his book, *Stuck!,* Terry Walling writes that Clinton studied "over three thousand historical, biblical and contemporary leaders." *Stuck!: Navigating the Transitions of Life and Leadership* (Apple Valley, MN: ChurchSmart Resources, 2008), vii.

The keystone project for all the students in Clinton's class was a biographical paper of their own life in relation to his theory of phases in the life of a leader. Ahead I will share how these phases played out in my own life—not because my story is outstanding or worthy of documenting, but because I want to pique your own recollection and realization of how elders or older ones have shaped your life, why you need them as you move forward, and why others need you as a Barnabas (an encourager) as well. As a start, think about the times you had those mentors and the times you needed them but had none.

For the health and welfare of our churches—with the collective intelligence of the body of Christ flowing at its best—we must purposefully recover the full function of true elders as mentors and encouragers. Like the Rosetans, we need to intentionally tap into the wisdom of the older ones.

Along the journey of our phases of life and ministry, we need older ones who are at least a phase or more ahead of us to offer wisdom and lessons from experience. Like a scout who says, "Listen, when you get past the second creek, you're going to have to go over a pass. As you descend that hill, take it easy. The rocks are loose, and you can lose your footing and take a tumble. Be patient on your way down."

Clinton's protégé, Terry Walling, describes five phases of lifelong development:[5]

| PHASE 1 Up to Early 20s | PHASE 2 Early 20s– Mid 30s | PHASE 3 Late 30s– Late 40s | PHASE 4 Mid 50s– Early 60s | PHASE 5 Early 60s |
|---|---|---|---|---|
| Sovereign Foundations | Inner-Life Growth | Ministry Maturing | Life Maturing | Convergence |

---

[5] Ibid., 77.

## Sovereign Foundations (up to early 20s)

Those of us raised in Christian families received training in doctrinal principles early on. Faith and scriptural foundations were initiated as God used family, environmental context, and events—both good and bad—to shape our character. The "primary lesson is to learn to respond positively and take advantage of what God has laid in these foundations."[6] During this phase, we often decide to follow Jesus and begin pursuing a relationship and understanding of the Lord—his ways, and his kingdom.

From this phase, I have tons of great memories of my grandad. Just about every other week, our family would drive an hour north and pass the weekend with my grandparents. We spent a lot of our summers with them as well. Every night, without fail, Grandad would turn off his bedside lamp and kneel beside the bed and pray. As the moonlight streamed through the window shades, I could see the figure of Grandad with hands clasped against his forehead, bent over the edge of the bed, praying. He gave thanks and praise to God for the day we just had—the morning we spent fishing on the banks of Blocker Creek or hunting squirrels near the old church's cemetery. He gave thanks for provision, for the fresh corn and okra, which the homestead garden yielded. He thanked the Lord for clothes and for a "place to rest our bodies"—a phrase I especially remember from his prayers, and that I hear myself praying to this day. Grandad gave thanks for his church and the fellowship they had formed. He asked God to forgive where he had sinned that day. Then he would ask the Lord to protect our family members—each by name. If there was a community or national issue, or a neighbor in crisis or need, he asked the Lord to attend to those concerns. I learned to pray from Grandad.

Because we visited so often, I grew up splitting Sundays between our Baptist church, near our home, and a little Nazarene church my grandparents, great uncles, aunts, and cousins were part of. By the time

---

[6]   Dr. J. Robert Clinton, *The Making of a Leader: Recognizing the Lessons and Stages of Leadership Development* (Carol Stream, IL: NavPress, 1988), 44.

I was twelve years old, I had absorbed quite a bit of Scripture. "Uncle Joe"—my grandma's older brother—was the patriarch of the extended family, and he would take me fishing and talk about the Lord and the Scriptures in between casts of the fishing line. We spent countless summer mornings on the front porch among my grandmother and her sisters (my great-aunts), snapping fresh green beans, listening to their stories and outlook on life—and soaking in wisdom from my matriarchs. These were the foundations God laid in my life.

The next phase of life is built upon those foundations.

## Inner-Life Growth (early 20s–mid-30s)

This phase is focused on developing a lifelong habit of prayer and having a listening ear. Discernment, understanding, and obedience are put to the test.

> The growing leader invariably gets involved in some form of ministry. In this phase, leadership potential is identified and God uses testing experiences to develop character. A proper, godly response allows a leader to learn the fundamental lessons God wants to teach. If the person doesn't learn, [they] will usually be tested again in the same areas. A proper response will result in an expanding ministry and greater responsibility.[7]

Several elders/encouragers strongly influenced me during this phase. As a young Bible-college student, it was Sam and Margie Spence who made a lasting impact that continues to yield fruit in my life. I mentioned Sam in an earlier chapter. The Spences' habit of being led by the Spirit is hard to adequately convey. The combination of their desire to hear and obediently respond to the Holy Spirit's guidance was like nothing I had ever experienced. I lost count of the number of times one of them would say, "Let's just stop and pray. Let's see what the Lord is saying here."

---

[7] Ibid., 45.

In relationship to my personal calling, Sam and Marge pushed me to speak and teach. They encouraged me by passing along books and tapes that had spoken to them. At times, they would caution me to slow down rather than rush to judgment or action. At other times they would let me push ahead in my fleshly ways only to return, tail between my legs, asking what the heck had just happened. Sam would grin and say, "Well, half-reverend [I was still in Bible college], how did that work out?" He would always help me out of the jam I had gotten myself—and sometimes him—into. Sam and Marge shared tons of stories and situations they had experienced in their own journey of life and ministry. There was rarely a season when they didn't have people living with them, usually someone who had reached a tough spot in life and needed a place to stay. They didn't just read the Bible. They lived it.

I started out on the typical "upward" track of ministry as a youth pastor and, after Bible college, I took a position at a church in West Texas. This was my first exposure to a dominating pastor. I was shocked to discover there were ministry leaders who believed the church was a business, and that to be successful, it should be run as such. I lasted six months there and returned to spend four more years under the mentorship of Sam and Marge.

In my late 20s, my wife and I moved to a small Missouri town called Rolla, and I was one pastor among a tribe of godly people, many of them much older than myself. The call to plant a church was stirring in me, and a small group of others joined in the dream. A group of us formed a fledgling startup team and, over a few years, we spent a lot of time with bona fide elders before heading out to plant a church.

The rhythm of life for us younger guys included frequent lunches, racquetball matches, impromptu prayer meetings, fishing trips, and coffee times with seasoned men. George, Dick, Terry, Gary, Dave, Mike, Royce, Gus, and others were our safe place. Their affable nature, decades of experience in church life, and longevity as faithful husbands and dedicated fathers had cultivated a wisdom that was a treasure trove we young guys could always draw from at a moment's notice. These men shared how they "worked out their salvation" as fathers, husbands, and in their businesses and among neighbors. They were an example of the Word being incarnated into real life.

None of those guys had ever served as paid members of a church staff. They came from a variety of blue- and white-collar vocations. Among them were a car salesman, a college professor, an electronics dealer, a forestry service worker, a bookkeeper, an orthodontist, and a cabinetmaker, as well as other trades and professions. But they all had gifts and callings that were every bit as sure as any church pro. Their APEST giftings spanned the range—apostolic, prophetic, evangelistic, pastoral; and they all could teach.

Our wives had their safe place as well. Older women were there for them—Suzi, Pat, Jane, Donna, Kay, Marjorie, and others provided a source of wisdom, encouragement, and hope along the journey of motherhood, marriage, discovering their own callings, using their gifts, and growing in patience and understanding in dealing with the goof-ups of young husbands.

Not only did the older men speak into the lives of the younger guys and the older women did likewise with the younger women, but they also offered priceless counsel as older couples to us younger couples. They were true elders. They had the ability and gravitas to help us grow, to calm us down when we thought the sky was falling, and to get out of the weeds when we found ourselves up to our necks in situations that were new to us.

## Ministry Maturing (late 30s–late 40s)

In this phase, the emerging leader begins to experiment with spiritual gifts they may or may not have been aware they were endowed with. They begin to zero in on their primary gifts and calling; and they experience an increased effectiveness, along with a better under-standing of the body of Christ as they encounter the many kinds of relationships it offers.[8] Both positive and negative experiences yield important lessons.

---

[8] Ibid., 45.

Walling says this is a transition whereby God works in us to:

- Surface uniqueness and contribution.
- Heal past wounding and deepen intimacy.
- Identify life messages and values.
- Provide better decision-making grids for future opportunities.
- Provide important first clues of ultimate contribution.[9]

When I first struck out to start a new church, I followed the advice of the writers and "experts" on church planting: I became *the Guy*. Cocksure and picking up the mantle of church-planter-Atlas, I leveraged all thirty years of my time on earth to start a church and function as the smartest guy in the room. Moving to our new place of calling in the Northwest suburbs of Saint Louis, Missouri, I led a small group of young, wide-eyed couples and singles. None of us had reached our forties yet, with most of us in our early thirties or younger.

Though we didn't realize it at the time, our team had been significantly cared for, mentored, and sent out by genuine elders; and we had little understanding of the full impact of this on our lives. The mother church we came from had been a haven. But now we were on our own. We didn't have the everyday availability of the wisdom of the older ones. Since we were young, we drew young singles and young couples to the new church. There were a few older people who came aboard, but we didn't view them as having much to say about the development and oversight of our church. *We* were the ones who had been trained in church planting. We were the young guns with the latest techniques and expertise in starting and running a church. After all, we knew how to set up smoke machines and put together PowerPoint slides.

The startup team included the couple who were best friends with my wife and me. John and Chris were on staff from the outset and played key roles. The four of us were incredibly tight. At the time, we were each raising three kids. Our children were all best friends as well.

---

[9]  Walling, *Stuck!*, 78.

They were in pairs, as we each had a child that had been born within months of one another. In short, our entire lives and ministry revolved around the connection of our two families. We even shared a house for the first year and a half of the new church start. Our friends and their children lived upstairs, and our family lived in the finished basement. I don't recommend it, but we miraculously had very little conflict and few problems.

Just under two years into starting the church, things were going gangbusters. The church was growing rapidly. We had purchased a property and were no longer doing mobile church. We had our own place. But the financial pressure was enormous. We were living week to week, and both the church and our families were getting by on a shoestring. The pressure was mounting, and our friends came to us one day and said they were leaving. He was joining his mother's business in another state. The decision was made. They could not see any chance that things were going to change anytime soon and had concluded that, if the church was relieved of the financial burden of them being on paid staff, it would help the church move forward as well as freeing them from the stress the church was under. We pleaded with them to reconsider and for us to all figure out a better solution, to no avail.

We were completely blindsided, having no clue they were considering this. But there was no talking them out of it. My wife and I were crushed. The entire dream for this church had been initiated and cultivated between the four of us. It was *our* dream. They were our best friends, our yokefellows. And in one brief afternoon meeting, it was all over. A couple of weeks later, tears streamed down the faces of our family—all five of us—as the moving van pulled away. I barely had the strength to raise an arm to wave goodbye.

It was the pressure that pushed them out. To be fair, in no small way, I had added to that pressure. Since I was still of the mindset that I was *the Guy*, I had made unilateral decisions that committed our church to financial obligations that we didn't have the margin to cover. Looking back, I am convinced that if there had been some elders in our lives locally, they would have been able to speak into the situation with wisdom, knowledge, and experience, and our friends very likely would have weathered the storm and stayed. If we had been functioning with elders rather than my shoot-from-the-hip tendencies, the storm would have been much milder. Over the next several years, the church grew— but it was never the same. We knew it would have been very different if John and Chris had stayed.

Eight years later, another transition happened—and I remember it well. We were ten years into the church we had planted, and I had just turned forty. It felt like a light switched off in me. Suddenly, I didn't want to continue pastoring this church I had given so much to and that had given so much to me. I felt like I was going crazy. There was no way I could envision leaving our church. I had just started building our dream house. My wife had the horses and animals she had yearned for from childhood. Our three kids were in their teens. Our church had just moved into a new building and had burgeoning children and youth ministries. Everything was good. Everything but me. I was in crisis. I needed counsel desperately.

By this time, we had established a team of elders, but they were all around the same age as me. Most of us were in a similar growth phase, and none of them had gone through the transition I was going through. There was no diversity of generational experience, so I didn't have the wisdom of the next generation to tap into.

Additionally, as with so many churches, our elders' role description revolved mostly around official church business, staffing, and policy issues. They didn't know how to handle or provide guidance for my situation, which appeared to be a combination of burnout and a mid-life crisis.

Around this time, I sat down with Bobby Clinton at his favorite booth in Coco's Bakery Restaurant, just off the Fuller Seminary campus in Pasadena. After sharing my angst, between bites of bacon and eggs, Bobby looked up from his plate and casually said, "Up to this point in your life, you thought you were doing what you were called to do. You thought you were *doing* ministry. But God has been *making* you a minister. The reality is that the Lord has been working in you to *prepare* you for what you are called to do. This is about your ultimate calling. Has there been fruitful ministry throughout your life? Sure. But if you choose to be faithful, your best days are ahead."

*What!* I thought to myself. *Do you mean to tell me everything I've done over the last ten years is not* real *ministry?* But that was not what he was saying. His point was that the Lord was doing something very normative and vital, but it was much deeper than I was aware of. Learning to exercise and experience the gifts the Lord distributes always yields fruit, but in his sovereignty, God is also working in us to help us reach our ultimate calling.

Terry Walling calls this phase a "Deciding Transition." Commonly called a mid-life crisis, this can be one of the most confusing times in our lives. Without receiving and applying wise counsel, it too often ends in disaster. Many people go off the rails in a desperate attempt to get out of what seems to be a dark place. Fortunately, I wasn't tempted to look for a red Corvette, another woman, or hair plugs and Botox to create a fresh start.

The reality is that this transition is a graduation portal. It's a commencement. The Lord is clarifying our ultimate calling and unique contribution, and the metamorphosis that takes place in this process challenges our identity. We thought our identity was in our talents and gifts, but the Lord shows us that our identity is actually as his sons, daughters, and servants. He is taking us from obsessing about *doing* to resting in *being*. He is shifting our drive from success to significance.

As Walling says, "Role is not about job or job descriptions. It is about the contribution an individual makes in each of the domains of life. Reduced to its core truth, role is coming to terms with what you do as a follower of Christ."[10] In this maturing phase, we are beginning the second half of life. Entrepreneur Bob Buford called it *Halftime* in his book by the same name.[11] We are deciding what to do with the

---

[10]  Ibid., 79.

[11]  Bob Buford, *Halftime: Moving from Success to Significance* (Grand Rapids, MI: Zondervan, 2015).

rest of our lives in light of our accumulated experience, wisdom, and knowledge. We have been given a toolkit from the Lord. The big questions are what we will do with it, and who can help us figure it out.

Up to this point in our lives, we have focused heavily on the activity of ministry—what we thought was most important, what we were made for. But as is so often the case, the Lord has a greater purpose. We thought he was primarily working *through* us while he was mostly working *on* us. The fruit of ministry is just an outcome of a deeper interior work taking place. We thought the Lord was growing an orange when all the while the Lord was producing seeds in the orange that would eventually become an orchard. Again, he is developing our *being* more than our *doing*.

The transition I was going through was toward my ultimate calling and gifting in more of a prophetic role. The problem was that my current identity was not only as *a* pastor but as *the* pastor. Besides not having a proper understanding of the importance and key roles of elders, none of us understood the beauty and vitality of the fivefold (APEST) gifts. Alan Hirsch explains the APEST gifts in this way:

> The apostle/apostolic is the quintessentially missional (from missio, the Latin equivalent) ministry ... the prophet/prophetic is the function tasked with maintaining an abiding loyalty and faithfulness to God above all ... the evangelist/evangelistic involves the proclamation of the good news that is at the core of the church's message ... the shepherd/shepherding is the function and calling responsible for maintaining and developing healthy community and enriching relationships ... the teacher/teaching is concerned with the mediation and appropriation of wisdom and understanding.[12]

In our context, I was always front and center. And when the guy doing most of the talking and leading begins to have an edge and is calling out issues that he is seeing from a prophetic eye, it throws a church into

---

[12] Hirsch, 5Q, xxxiii–xxxiv.

confusion. *What happened to Pastor Lance?* people were wondering. I was trying to be a pastor but was becoming something else.

When we started the church, I was functioning in an apostolic role. The core group that starts a new church, and the people who initially join that church, tend to be early adopters who catch on quickly to the entrepreneurial voice of the apostolic. But as a church grows, people need the heart, wisdom, and voice of a shepherd. Although I gave it my best shot as a pastor, it was not my strength. If the team doesn't have shepherds, the solo church planter, who has functioned as an apostle early on, either must transition toward the pastor role or must make way for those who have that gift in significant measure. This doesn't mean the church planter must move on, but he or she must make room for other gifted leaders.

There *were* people in my church who were more gifted with the heart and insight of a shepherd, but our paradigm of leadership—one person at the top—offered no place for them. I was starting new things, changing things up on a whim, spending increasing amounts of time training young church planters, as well as thinking more and more prophetically. It was frustrating and confusing for all of us. I was still leading apostolically, but I was taking up pastoral space that others were more gifted for.

Bobby Clinton's counsel—my only outside voice of wisdom at that time—was indeed clarifying for me. But a lot of grief could have been avoided if I had been doing life among a group of elders who had gone through the phase I was currently going through. I know there were many other men and women in our church experiencing similar transitions, but our paradigm of eldership offered nothing to help them navigate those waters. By this time, our church had grown to a point where there were several older couples on board who had decades of life experience and wisdom, but our church wasn't tapping into it. Our system disrupted the connections between the brain and body. We were heavy on rank-based titles that limited input and authority to speak into situations and decisions. The headship of Jesus and the disseminated wisdom into the body of Christ were interrupted by our structure. We were out of whack with our true Atlas.

## Life Maturing (mid 50s–early 60s)

Those who have reached this phase and are faithfully walking it out have discovered and identified their unique calling and accompanying spiritual gifts. Their greatest desire is communion with God, and "success" in ministry is set aside as the primary goal. They are learning "the unforced rhythms of grace" (see Matthew 11:28–30 MSG). Less effort is yielding a more beautiful dance. Incredibly, the faithful leader in this phase experiences their greatest period of fruitfulness. He or she "gains a sense of priorities concerning the best use of [their] gifts and understands that learning what not to do is as important as learning what to do. A mature fruitfulness is the result."[13] It is a counterintuitive outcome. Just like shifting gears on a bicycle—moving from a lower gear to a higher one—those in this stage are using less effort but are gaining more ground.

I witnessed the fruit of this phase in Bobby Clinton's life. I was once working on the speaker lineup for a conference and needed an expert on mentoring for a main session. It just so happened I was scheduled to be at Fuller Seminary for an intensive class over a week, so I arranged to meet with Bobby to tap into his wisdom on a couple of personal issues and to invite him to speak. I was certain he would say yes. When I told Bobby about the conference and asked him to partic-ipate, he said, "No. I won't do that. I've found that more fruit comes out of spending my time one-on-one with young folks like I'm doing with you today, or with the little group of twelve guys and gals I'm mentoring. Thanks, but I'll pass." He was foregoing the opportunity to speak to around five hundred pastors and leaders. But Bobby was no longer interested in pursuing what most of us would call success. His focus was significance.

---

[13] Clinton, *The Making of a Leader*, 46.

The Life Maturing phase yields true *spiritual authority*—not from rank, privilege, title, platform, or position, but from one's being. It doesn't have to be commanded or demanded. It's just there. And those around people with true spiritual authority don't fear it; they lean into it. They feel the safety of it and desire to learn from it. It is superior to positional power because it touches people's hearts rather than forces people's hands. Elders at this stage don't exude power; they emit spiritual authority that is a byproduct of life experience and abiding in Christ. They have an air of encouraging influence rather than towering intimidation.

## Convergence (somewhere in 60s)

This is the era when everything seems to make the most sense in one's calling—when everything comes together. God brings a person "into a role that matches his or her gift-mix and experience so that ministry is maximized,"[14] and he or she experiences an even deeper sense of ease of ministry. Life maturing and ministry maturing converge so the person becomes most effective in the lives of others. Life itself becomes the ultimate response to a lifelong commitment to abiding in Christ.

Walling shares that during this season, God purposes to:

- Inspire and challenge followers with the notion of finishing well.
- Move a follower into the convergence of being and doing.
- Solidify a follower's clarity as to ultimate contribution and legacy.
- Bring together lessons and experiences of past wounds and successes.
- Dispense an increased spiritual authority to serve others.
- Identify protégés who can be entrusted with one's insights and learning.[15]

My encouragement is for church leaders to identify men and women (or pray for some to show up) who are in the Convergence stage. It's

---

[14] Ibid.

[15] Walling, *Stuck!*, 87.

helpful to make them known and noticed among the fellowship so that their gifts can be seen and accessed.

## YOUR STORY

As you were reading this section, hopefully your own journey came to mind. Look back over each of the five stages we have just covered and consider these questions:

- In which seasons, if any, did you have elders or older ones to walk alongside you?
- If no one was available to mentor you, how do you imagine you could have been helped if someone had been there in your life?
- Which phase are you currently in?
- Are there older ones who regularly speak into your life today?
- Are there younger ones, currently in a stage you have gone through, for whom you do or could provide an elder voice?

Hopefully, you are catching on that far from implying younger ones are not fit to lead, I am suggesting that the latent treasure in genuine elders is needed alongside younger leaders. The energy and risk-taking imagination of the younger ones in tandem with the wisdom and experience of the older ones not only makes sense, but it is also God's plan and provision.

The issue is that we too often have left it to young men and women to start and lead new churches primarily on their own. This leaves them deprived of the support and encouragement of seasoned men and women who can make an enormous impact on their lives and the whole church.

Let me share a bit more about what took place in the ministry that sent me and our team to plant a church. Not only were the elders of that ministry there for us as a church-planting team, but they also formed the backbone of their church. Years before I had joined them, this mother church had experienced several seasons without an "official" pastor. During those times, they had no vocational pastors whatsoever. So how did the church make it through such "pastorless" seasons? They actually thrived.

A few years ago, I came across some cassette tapes (Google it, millennials) from the Sunday services during this church's last season without a pastor. It was amazing to soak in the wisdom the elders led from. They oversaw the church incredibly well. They taught the body, initiated hospitality and fellowship, and provided encouragement, hope, and comfort when needed. How can I sum up what those elders did? I know of no other way to put it than they *elded*. And they did it well! They used their own APEST gifts "[to equip] the saints for the work of ministry, for building up the body of Christ" (Ephesians 4:12). As a team of vocationally called ones came on board, the church was in a healthy state and in a good place to move forward.

My father-in-law was one of those elders, and I watched from afar how he and the other elders functioned during these transitional seasons. He told me, "Those were some really hard times, but on the other hand, they were good times. We really didn't know what we were doing. We just did it." This is a beautiful picture of *doing* coming from *being*. Seasoned men and women—elders—functioned as overseers. They were members of the body of Christ who were connecting with the Head of the church, Jesus—and the wisdom of the Head flowed through them throughout the body.

Best of all, when the church transitioned out of the "pastorless" phase, the elders did not return to the sidelines and turn everything over to the pros. They continued to function as overseers.

## THE "POSITION" OF AN ELDER

A lot of things come to mind when we think about the elders of a church. As I mentioned earlier in this chapter, in many new churches, the elders are just the most mature young people among a lot of other young people. In many established churches, the elders are a board of successful businesspeople. They know how to run a business or corporation, so it seems to make sense they are the best choice to *run* a church. But what do we find in the New Testament? (Verse numbers are included here because we'll look at them in detail below.)

> ¹ So I exhort the elders among you, as a fellow elder and a witness of the sufferings of Christ, as well as a partaker in the glory that is going to be revealed: ² shepherd the flock of God that is among you, exercising oversight, not under compulsion, but willingly, as God would have you; not for shameful gain, but eagerly; ³ not domineering over those in your charge, but being examples to the flock. ⁴ And when the chief Shepherd appears, you will receive the unfading crown of glory. ⁵ Likewise, you who are younger, be subject to the elders. Clothe yourselves, all of you, with humility toward one another, for "God opposes the proud but gives grace to the humble."
>
> 1 PETER 5:1–5

Let's look more closely at this passage:

### "I exhort the elders *among* you" (v. 1, emphasis mine)

In this letter, Peter is writing to the saints throughout the Roman provinces of Asia Minor. He is speaking directly to the body of Christ, not to any official leaders of the churches. Here in chapter five, Peter directs his words to the elders who are "among" the saints. This is their *position*, but it is not an office they hold. The elders are shoulder to shoulder, not "over" anyone in a ranking office. They are co-laborers, fellow servants, and brothers and sisters. The elders are embedded within the body of Christ. It is erroneous to think of elders in terms of offices. The New Testament contains no Greek word for "office." To think of church elders as officeholders is to superimpose our own notions, preconceived ideas, or preferences upon the text.

*"Shepherd* the flock of God that is among you" (v. 2, emphasis mine)
The first order for elders is to function as pastors. They are to feed and care for the flock. A key requirement for those recognized as elders is also the ability to teach (1 Timothy 3:2). In his letter to Titus, Paul tells him what to look for in an elder. He says the elder must "have a good grip on the Message, knowing how to use the truth to either spur people on in knowledge or stop them in their tracks if they oppose it (Titus 1:9 MSG). The body of Christ exists in a malnourished state in part because we believe the job of feeding and caring for the church is the task of one or two paid professionals. Not only is the task impossible, but it was also never God's plan. The flock is to be shepherded by all the elders who are already among the flock.

**"Exercising** *oversight"* (v. 2, emphasis mine)
Some translations say, "serving as overseers." This is the overall role of an elder/shepherd. The Greek word is *episkopéō*: to look upon, inspect, oversee, look after, care for. As we will see shortly, there is no hint of domineering or headship in this role. This is about loving care and keeping a tender and watchful eye of protection over the flock—the very thing a shepherd does for their sheep.

**"Not under compulsion, but willingly"** (v. 2)
The word for "compulsion" here means "constraint" or "force." Overseeing is not about the exercise of power and position.

**"Not for shameful gain, but eagerly"** (v. 2)
Peter exhorts elders to oversee not for money, which would make them hirelings, but out of service to the Lord. It is also not to be pursued for status or power. This is not a professional position. It is to be undertaken with a willing heart motivated by love for the body of Christ.

**"Not** *domineering* **over those in your charge"** (v. 3, emphasis mine)
The word used for "domineering" here is the same word Jesus used in Mark 10:42 when Jesus commanded his disciples that they were not

to be like the Gentiles who practiced leadership through domination. Peter surely was remembering the words of Jesus. How could he forget the day the Lord took the disciples to task for hinting at their own desire for future power in his coming kingdom (Luke 22:24–27)?

**"But being *examples* to the flock" (v. 3, emphasis mine)**
Elders are to have a character and life that is worth imitating. Scattered throughout the church, we should have older men and women who not only speak to us through their words but also through their lives. When we look at Jim and Emily or Dave and Becky, we should think, *This is what following Jesus should look like.*

Elders are overseers and shepherds. They are neither overlords nor senior shepherds. Overseeing is never to be overlording in the church. The saints already have a Lord. Elders are among the flock of Jesus, who is the one and only Lord and Chief Shepherd—the very title Peter uses for Jesus in the next verse (1 Peter 5:4). Elders watch out for the spiritual health of the body. They care for the needs of the flock, being commissioned by the Chief Shepherd—Senior Pastor, Jesus Christ.

As v. 2 specified, elders are the ones who *over-see*. The word *episkopéō* comes from a conjunction of two words: over and scope. Through decades of walking with God, they have honed a clear eye for looming problems. They stand as watchpersons on the wall, seeing what is "out there" beyond the view of those below. They are not supervisors, but they have a sense of super-vision. They are not *over* in a sense of superiority, but in a sense of seeing. Their oversight is a discernment that often allows them to see situations with a clarity that younger ones may not have. Speaking about the role of first-century elders, Frank Viola writes in *Reimagining Church*, "They had their spiritual antennae continually raised to check for wolves. As older [ones], their wisdom was sought after in times of crisis. And when they spoke, their voices possessed the weight of experience."[16]

---

[16]  Viola, *Reimagining Church*, 171.

## THE WITNESS OF THE NEW TESTAMENT: THE "APPOINTMENT" OF ELDERS

The role and importance of elders in a local church might be best understood by looking at the frequency with which they appear in the scriptural account. Throughout my thirty-plus years of involvement in church planting, I have read myriad books and been involved in hundreds of seminars and conferences on church planting and leadership. The mention or emphasis of the importance of older ones or elders is scant at best. When it is covered, eldership is portrayed most often as a seat at a table of decision-makers.

If we want to see churches that the "gates of hell" don't prevail against (see Matthew 16:18), then it needs to be Jesus who is building them and not us who are constructing them from our own blueprints. How have we done so? In the Gospels, we see the term "disciple" mentioned over 260 times. We see "church" mentioned in two verses. There is no arguing against the fact that we have focused on church development and treated disciple-making as an add-on. The term "pastor" is used one time in the New Testament (Ephesians 4:11), but we are pretty obsessed with it. The word "leader" is used only two times in the New Testament—once referring to Jesus as Leader (Acts 5:31) and the other time uttered as Jesus is correcting his disciples for their desire for hierarchy. In his rebuke, Jesus defines a leader as a servant (Luke 22:26). Just ask yourself: When was the last time you heard of a "servant conference"? In the book of Revelation, we see elders mentioned in the account of the triumphant church a dozen times. There is no mention of pastors. No mention of leaders. Yet, what do we focus on?

Elders in a local context are mentioned twenty times from Acts through 1 Peter (emphases mine):

And they did so, sending it [the letter] to the *elders* by the hand of Barnabas and Saul.

ACTS 11:30

And when they had appointed *elders* for them in every church, with prayer and fasting they committed them to the Lord in whom they had believed.

ACTS 14:23

And after Paul and Barnabas had no small dissension and debate with them, Paul and Barnabas and some of the others were appointed to go up to Jerusalem to the apostles and the *elders* about this question.

ACTS 15:2

When they came to Jerusalem, they were welcomed by the church and the apostles and the *elders*, and they declared all that God had done with them.

ACTS 15:4

The apostles and the *elders* were gathered together to consider this matter.

ACTS 15:6

Then it seemed good to the apostles and the *elders*, with the whole church, to choose men from among them and send them to Antioch with Paul and Barnabas. They sent Judas called Barsabbas, and Silas, leading men among the brothers.

ACTS 15:22

The brothers, both the apostles and the *elders*, to the brothers who are of the Gentiles in Antioch and Syria and Cilicia, greetings.

ACTS 15:23

As they went on their way through the cities, they delivered to them for observance the decisions that had been reached by the apostles and *elders* who were in Jerusalem.

ACTS 16:4

Now from Miletus he sent to Ephesus and called the *elders* of the church to come to him.

ACTS 20:17

On the following day Paul went in with us to James, and all the *elders* were present.

ACTS 21:18

[T]he high priest and the whole council of *elders* can bear me witness. From them I received letters … and I journeyed toward Damascus to take those also who were there and bring them in bonds to Jerusalem to be punished.

ACTS 22:5

They went to the chief priests and *elders* and said, "We have strictly bound ourselves by an oath to taste no food till we have killed Paul."

ACTS 23:14

And after five days the high priest Ananias came down with some *elders* and a spokesman, one Tertullus. They laid before the governor their case against Paul.

ACTS 24:1

And when I was at Jerusalem, the chief priests and the *elders* of the Jews laid out their case against him, asking for a sentence of condemnation against him.

ACTS 25:15

Do not neglect the gift you have, which was given you by prophecy when the council of *elders* laid their hands on you.

1 TIMOTHY 4:14

Let the *elders* who rule well be considered worthy of double honor, especially those who labor in preaching and teaching.

1 TIMOTHY 5:17

This is why I left you in Crete, so that you might put what remained into order, and appoint *elders* in every town as I directed you.

TITUS 1:5

Is anyone among you sick? Let him call for the *elders* of the church, and let them pray over him, anointing him with oil in the name of the Lord.

JAMES 5:14

So I exhort the *elders* among you, as a fellow elder and a witness of the sufferings of Christ, as well as a partaker in the glory that is going to be revealed.

1 PETER 5:1

Likewise, you who are younger, be subject to the *elders*. Clothe yourselves, all of you, with humility toward one another, for "God opposes the proud but gives grace to the humble."

1 PETER 5:5

In our current church structures, we have two types of elders. Some of them are older ones in the faith community who have not been appointed to oversee a particular group or department; they are simply members of the community. They are God's wisdom bearers, his distributed intelligence in the body.

Others have been appointed or ordained. We make a big deal out of ordination in our churches and denominations today, but there are only two instances in the New Testament where the ordination of elders appears. Paul tells Titus, who was serving in Crete, to appoint elders (Titus 1:5). The Greek word is *kathistēmi*. It means "to constitute, to declare, show to be." There is no place where ministers (servants) or pastors are ordained or appointed. We only see it used in relationship to elders.

When Paul instructs Titus to ordain elders, he is saying it as a way to highlight them, to publicly acknowledge their value to the church, and to declare that they are a gift to the body. The other place elders are ordained is Acts 14:23, when Paul and Barnabas appointed elders in the regional churches they were working with. The Greek word here is *cheirotoneō*, which means "to stretch out the hand." They laid hands on these elders as a public acknowledgment of the Lord's work in and gifting of these older ones to the church. In essence, they were saying to the church, "Look what a gift we have here in these folks! Let's pull the bow and wrapping paper off and unbox it!"

We find no *office* of "senior pastor" in Scripture. Yet, we do indeed have senior pastors. They are older ones with pastoral giftings. Elders are people of seasoned *character* who function as *overseers* and are gifted as *shepherds*.[17] They are a gift beyond measure to the body of Christ. Tap into their gifts. Draw from their wisdom. Pull them off the bench and put them into the game!

In closing, please understand that some younger men and women carry elder wisdom, so we need these younger elders as well. As we consider who the elders are in our midst, it is incumbent on us to look for a diversity of age, gender, and ethnicity that represents the way we are fearfully and wonderfully made in God's own image—the totality of his image. We need the vigor and vision of the younger gifted ones alongside the wisdom and experience of the older ones. We need the insight and sensibilities of women and the perspective of people of color. If we have such diversity in our faith community, we would do well to seek it in our elders as well. To fail in this regard is to circumvent the wisdom of the Head. To make these connections certain and true is a vital step toward the realignment and restoration of the wisdom circuits of the entire body.

---

[17] Ibid., 170.

# For Teams to Process

- **Identification of Eldership**
  - How do we currently identify and recognize potential elders within our congregation?
  - To what extent, are we open to diverse candidates for eldership in terms of age, gender, ethnicity, and background?

- **Appointment and Ordination**
  - What is our process for appointing and ordaining elders? Is it clear and transparent?
  - In what ways do we publicly acknowledge and celebrate the gifting and wisdom of our elders during the ordination process?

- **Role and Responsibilities**
  - How do we define the role and responsibilities of elders within our church? Is it consistent with the New Testament model?
  - Are elders primarily seen as decision-makers, or do they actively shepherd and provide wisdom to the congregation?

- **Diversity and Inclusivity**
  - How diverse is our current group of elders in terms of age, gender, ethnicity, and background?
  - In what ways are we actively seeking out and engaging potential elders who may bring unique perspectives and giftings to the leadership team?

- **Leadership Development**
  - What is our current program or process

for developing potential elders within our congregation?

- How are we mentoring and equipping younger individuals with elder-like wisdom and character?

- **Recognition of Wisdom and Experience**
  - To what extent do we value the wisdom and experience of our elder leaders?
  - How are we actively seeking their counsel and guidance in decision-making and pastoral care?

- **Reevaluation of Terminology**
  - In what ways could we reevaluate the terminology used in our church, such as "senior pastor," to better align with the biblical model of eldership?
  - What changes in terminology could help clarify the roles and responsibilities of leaders within our congregation?

- **Leadership Alignment**
  - How closely does our current leadership structure align with the principles of eldership as outlined in the New Testament?
  - What adjustments or realignments are needed to better reflect the biblical model?

- **Community Engagement**
  - How are we engaging potential elders within our church community?
  - What opportunities are there for them to serve and lead alongside current elders?

- **Feedback and Listening**
  - In what ways are we actively seeking feedback from the congregation about the role and effectiveness of our eldership?
  - To what extent do we listen to the concerns and suggestions of our church members regarding elder leadership?

- **Continual Improvement**
  - What steps can we take to continually improve our understanding and practice of eldership within our church?
  - What resources, training, or outside guidance could help us enhance our eldership model?

- **Prayer and Discernment**
  - How are we seeking God's guidance and discernment in the selection and activation of elders within our congregation?
  - To what extent are we dedicating time to prayer and seeking the Holy Spirit's direction in this important process?

# 8

# RESTRUCTURING AND REHABILITATING THE BODY

## Practical Matters and Next Steps

*God grabbed me. God's Spirit took me up and set me down in the middle of an open plain strewn with bones. He led me around and among them—a lot of bones! There were bones all over the plain—dry bones, bleached by the sun. He said to me, "Son of man, can these bones live?" I said, "Master God, only you know that." He said to me, "Prophesy over these bones: 'Dry bones, listen to the Message of God!'" God, the Master, told the dry bones, "Watch this: I'm bringing the breath of life to you and you'll come to life. I'll attach sinews to you, put meat on your bones, cover you with skin, and breathe life into you. You'll come alive and you'll realize that I am God!"*

EZEKIEL 37:1–6 MSG

Sometimes we love change. At other times we hate it. When we find ourselves in pain, discontented, frustrated, or even depressed, change can give us hope. But sometimes we are so tired or lacking in faith, we don't have the energy for change. Meaningful change seldom comes without a cost, but refusing to change can be more damaging in the long run. If you have read this far into the book, I'm assuming you are not only convinced that changes need to be made in your leadership culture, but you are also up for the challenge.

Change is essential if the church is to see a fruitful future. In today's culture, the church is constantly facing challenges that require solutions beyond our current knowledge. This reality is called an "adaptive challenge"—a circumstance that demands we change, or we will become bound to, or even die from, the situation we are presently in. The COVID-19 pandemic was a worldwide physical, economic, and social adaptive challenge.

You may have personally experienced some type of physical ailment that presented you with an adaptive challenge. It may have been a vehicle accident, a fall, an illness, or something else that affected your body. When I was twenty-five years old, I blew out my left knee in a church softball game. Both my ACL and MCL ligaments completely snapped, as well as the meniscus. Was I going to die from the injury? No, but it was crippling. If it had happened in 1889 rather than in 1989, I would have been limping for the rest of my life. Thankfully, a skilled surgeon rebuilt my knee. But then it was up to me to put in the excruciatingly hard work over the next nine months to start walking, running, and competing athletically again. That part is called "rehab." We cannot read or conference our way into rebuilding and rehabilitation. We must put in the hard work.

## THE REALIGNMENT PROCESS

Let's look at a few of the action steps involved in rehabbing and realigning the body of Christ to Jesus as Head.

### Repent

To repent is to change one's heart and mind. It is admitting that we are going in the wrong direction; that we are on the wrong track, and we need to turn around. At times, we feel penitent to the point of tears. Nowhere in Scripture are we told that weeping is required for repentance, but sometimes as we reflect on the cost to others or ourselves because of our misdirection or misdeeds, we are indeed overcome with a sense of deep brokenness. Either way, tears or not, the one sure sign of repentance is a determined change of direction. Repentance without a conscious decision to switch directions is disingenuous.

True *metanoia* (the Greek word for "repentance") is always evidenced by a turnaround. Just imagine if I were driving to your house and failed to show up on time. You called to check on me, and I told you the GPS told me to do a U-turn, but I ignored it. You would probably demand an explanation. If I told you I ignored the GPS because my car was running great, and I really liked the direction I was going, I was enjoying the scenery, and my favorite hamburger joint was up ahead, you would either think I was just plain crazy or that I just didn't care about seeing you.

It is impossible to repent and keep going in the same direction, to keep doing what we have been doing. The Lord calls us to prove our change of heart by a change in the way we proceed. "Therefore produce fruit consistent with repentance" (Matthew 3:8 NASB).

As we have seen thus far, the damage caused by the prevailing leadership systems in the modern-day church is incalculable. Those who choose to repent do not do so because leadership hasn't *worked;* they do so because they recognize they've been part of a system of rebellion against God. We repent for our disobedience and for building our own kingdoms and Towers of Babel. We call it out for what it is, and we hold ourselves responsible for our actions. We have rejected God, refuted and ignored Jesus' words and path, and chosen our own way. When we truly come to grips with these facts, it should bring us to a place not only of deep sorrow and brokenness but also of change.

## Be Patient

It is typically the apostolic and prophetically gifted persons who sense a need for change and find themselves intrigued by a new, fresh idea. When we sense that spark, those of us who fall into these categories usually throw ourselves into reading everything we can; attending every conference, seminar, or training experience we can find; and then regurgitating that excitement all over the people we are journeying with. And we quickly become frustrated when they do not "get it" or push back on what we see so *clearly*.

We forget the journey we have taken to arrive at a new understanding and are anxious to move this thing along as rapidly as possible. We become impatient, and our agitation can easily irritate those around us. We have to remember that our understanding evolved through thinking, reading, and praying, and it is God's grace that has brought us to this place. Other people deserve time and space to reorient their own thinking and come to see our point of view.

As we attempt to move into a new approach to leadership, it helps to remember that change is much more likely to happen if we understand and lean into our interdependence; if we trust and rely on our team members who have different giftings. In any group or organization, change is diffused throughout the members who make up the body of the group. Healing change works its way through the body. It does not happen because someone at the top declares it to be so. This is especially true for the church. Again, think *body*, not business.

I've referred before to "early adopters" and "innovators." These terms come from a theory developed by professor of communication studies Everett Rogers called "diffusion of innovations"—which helps to explain the dynamics of how new ideas and technology spread throughout any group or organization. In his book *Diffusion of Innovations*, Rogers identifies five types of people that you might be familiar with: *innovators, early adopters, early majority, late majority*, and *laggards*.[1]

Many apostles are innovators. They start things because they typically see ahead of the curve. Similarly, many prophets are early adopters. They scout the land ahead and report back to the larger group. Both innovators and early adopters are enthusiastic about what they see and the possibilities at hand. But they can easily overwhelm and even alarm the rest of the body, who have not yet seen what the

---

[1] Everett Rogers, *Diffusion of Innovations* (New York, NY: Macmillan, 1962).

innovators and early adopters are convinced of. They are often accused of having a "ready, fire, aim" modus operandi. If the innovators/apostles and the early adopters/prophets are not wise, patient, and sensitive as they push the agenda toward what they indeed are seeing correctly, they can cause a lot of turmoil.

Far too often, when a change is proposed, it comes as an announcement from the top-ranking leaders. Interestingly enough, the first step toward transforming the culture is to shift the way change happens. If your church or organization has been top-down, the first order of change is not to modify the top-down structure by using top-down methods. What irony!

A new trail is made by walking it. Put another way, we act our way into a new way of thinking. We tend to *teach* our way into new ways of thinking. That is certainly a part of the process, but it is just *part* of it. Including and relying upon the other APEST members in the process is not only vital but also much more peaceful, effective, and fun.

To further illustrate this process, look at the diagram on the next page. Rogers's research revealed that for change to take place in a group or organization made up of people with a variety of comfort levels, change cannot be commanded—it must be "diffused" slowly. In any culture, 2.5 percent of the members are innovators, and 13.5 percent are early adopters who catch on to the new concepts quickly. Those in this early majority make up just over one-third of the group—34 percent. The late majority is another third of the group. It takes a while before they are convinced of change. At the far right of the spectrum are what Rogers labeled as laggards, an unfortunate term. This 16 percent of the populace is strongly hesitant to change of just about any kind. They sometimes seem to want everything left as it is, including the dust that has collected!

Rogers's theory is that as we move from left to right across the spectrum, it is the ones to the immediate left that have the most influence on the ones to their immediate right. For example, the late majority are not heavily persuaded by innovators or early adopters. In their view, those people are always coming up with something new and do not sufficiently think things through. Instead, those in the late majority are influenced by those in the early majority. Those in the early majority are mostly influenced by early adopters, and so on. If we want to see change in church leadership structures, we cannot change them using our old power structures. We must have patience as change is quickly embraced by the innovators and early adopters, but then slowly "diffused" throughout the rest of the body.

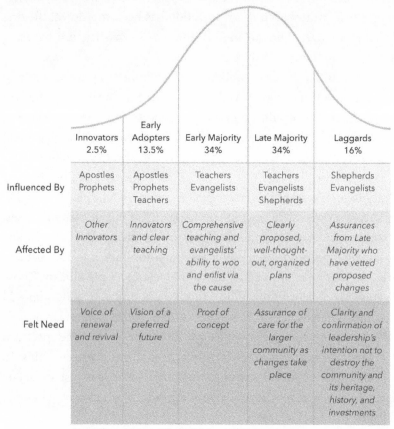

| | Innovators 2.5% | Early Adopters 13.5% | Early Majority 34% | Late Majority 34% | Laggards 16% |
|---|---|---|---|---|---|
| Influenced By | Apostles Prophets | Apostles Prophets Teachers | Teachers Evangelists | Teachers Evangelists Shepherds | Shepherds Evangelists |
| Affected By | *Other Innovators* | *Innovators and clear teaching* | *Comprehensive teaching and evangelists' ability to woo and enlist via the cause* | *Clearly proposed, well-thought-out, organized plans* | *Assurances from Late Majority who have vetted proposed changes* |
| Felt Need | *Voice of renewal and revival* | *Vision of a preferred future* | *Proof of concept* | *Assurance of care for the larger community as changes take place* | *Clarity and confirmation of leadership's intention not to destroy the community and its heritage, history, and investments* |

Adapted from: E. Rogers, *Diffusion of Innovations* (1962)

It is important to pay close attention to the differing voices from the diversity of gifts of those in the space. For instance, when a major change is initiated, it is the shepherds and teachers who will be most influential in bringing along those in the late majority because these are the folks who need assurance that the community is not in danger of being hurt or destroyed. The apostles and prophets on your team are less likely to bring this assurance. In fact, they may well come across so forcefully that it confirms and fortifies the fears of the late majority. The genuine guidance of a true shepherd and the thorough information provided by the teacher may delay progress in the minds of the apostles, prophets, and evangelists, but it often brings about a more prayerful and thoughtful approach to the proposed changes.

## Get an Examination

When we are seriously ill or incapacitated, we need the help of medical professionals who start by assessing what is going on with our bodies. They will do blood tests, MRIs, CT scans, X-rays, and other such tests to get an accurate understanding of our present condition. The results of these exams help to reveal what is both functional and dysfunctional in our body's systems. For instance, after a thorough examination, a doctor might sit down and tell us the results of our blood work. "Your cholesterol numbers look great and so do the figures on your kidney function," she may report. "But I don't like what I am seeing in your liver function." She may recommend more tests or a treatment plan to get your body back to full health.

In recent years, many effective assessments have been developed to help churches get an unbiased picture of the state of their health in various key areas. When I work with teams on issues of leadership, one of the first things I ask them to do is to participate in some combination of assessments, including those we have developed.[2] Again, your team is the body of Christ, and therefore multiple members must be involved in the assessments in order to determine a pathway for vibrant leadership health for the future.

---

[2] For example, I have developed assessments for use in training systems such as The Starfish and The Spirit Lab, https://www.thestarfishandthespirit.com/accelerator.

Catalytic leaders understand the gifts, passions, and stories of their team members. This awareness increases the possibility of a meaningful interdependent dance, where a team moves together, leveraging each person's strengths and buttressing each other's weaknesses. Without assessments, however, the dance diminishes as we step on each other's toes. The following are some examples of helpful assessments:

- GPS: Gifts, Passion, Story (giftspassionstory.com)
- DiSC profile (discprofile.com)
- CliftonStrengths (gallup.com/cliftonstrengths)
- 5 Voices (5voices.com)
- Enneagram (enneagraminstitute.com)
- APEST (5qcentral.com)
- mDNA Assessment (themxplatform.com)

## Recognize Your Resources

One of the most encouraging things that happens following proper assessments is that leaders discover that they have many more assets than they previously realized. When we unstack our hierarchies, we effectively unleash and unshackle many gifted persons the Lord has provided for the mission we are called to. Moving to a form of peer-based, decentralized leadership releases untapped power through people who have been there all along but were sidelined. The collective intelligence of the whole becomes available and set in motion. The body will heal itself and begin functioning healthily when we get our systems right.

This is where faith must be engaged. Think about it. If the Lord Jesus is truly building his church—a church you are a part of—then he has provided gifted men and women to get the job done (Ephesians 4). There is only one Master Builder. It is either you (or some other human) at the top, or it is Jesus. If it is a human, the enterprise is doomed to failure. If it is Jesus, it can't fail!

When the body becomes aligned with its true Atlas, the body's other members start working together and do what they are meant to do. APEST gifts kick into gear; true elders start functioning; and the wisdom, knowledge, and understanding from the Holy Spirit is multiplied throughout the church and team (staff) members. The hard yoke and heavy burden of human leadership methods yield to the easy yoke and light burden of realignment to Jesus' ways.

One helpful resource in this process is *Find Your Place: Locating Your Calling Through Your Gifts, Passions, and Story* by Rob Wegner and Brian Phipps.[3] This book helps individuals and teams discover and activate the gifts and callings that are present but possibly lying dormant. Visit www.giftspassionstory.com, where you can find resources to help with full implementation in your context.

In addition to the assessments listed above, here are a few potential activities for team members to use in processing their personal calling.

- **Gifts assessment:** Ask everyone to complete a gifts assessment tool to help them identify their natural and spiritual gifts. This could be a self-assessment questionnaire, or it could involve seeking input from friends, family, or other trusted individuals. Ask everyone to reflect on the results of the assessment and consider how their gifts might fit into their sense of calling and purpose in life, as well as that of the church or organization.
- **Passion exploration:** Ask everyone to spend some time exploring their areas of interest. This could involve brainstorming a list of activities or causes that they are passionate about, or it could include trying out new activities or volunteering in order to discover new interests. Make time for them to reflect with the larger team or their department team on what they are learning about their passions and how they might relate to their sense of calling and purpose in life.
- **Personal story reflection:** Ask members to spend some time

---

[3] Rob Wegner and Brian Phipps, *Find Your Place: Locating Your Calling Through Your Gifts, Passions, and Story* (Grand Rapids, MI: Zondervan, 2019).

reflecting on their personal stories and the events and experiences that have shaped their lives. This could involve writing a personal narrative or creating a timeline of significant events. Ask them to consider how their personal story fits into the larger narrative of God's work in their lives and how it might help the church or organization fulfill its mission.

- **Calling plan:** Ask each person to use what they have learned about their gifts, passions, and personal stories to develop a plan for pursuing their calling and purpose in life. This could involve setting goals, identifying practical steps to take, or creating a vision statement for their calling. Ask each team member to present their plans to the team and discuss how their calling plans align with their gifts, passions, and personal stories.

## Learn a New Language

Once we have recognized all the unique gifts in the body, we must learn a new language that highlights giftings rather than position or status. As has been stressed throughout this book, terminology and titles have an enormous influence in shaping an organizational culture. Each and every day, for good or bad, the terms we use nudge us one way or the other. Getting the language right will go a long way in constantly keeping the spinal column of our church bodies in alignment with our Head—Jesus.

Get creative with your titles and terms. For example, take the term "director." We know what this means. The director of any area in a church or organization is the "boss" of that domain. If we are serious about realignment, such terms are unhelpful. They pinch the nerves of alignment each time they are uttered or read. Why not use the term "equipper"? Why have a small groups director when we can have a small groups equipper? Wouldn't you rather have a missions equipper than a missions director? A director *tells* others *what* to do. An equipper *trains* and *resources* others on *how* to do things.

| Old Language | New Language |
|---|---|
| Boss | Coach/mentor |
| Director | Equipper |
| Employee | Coworker/peer |
| Leader | Servant |

Taking a language audit of your leadership culture can be invaluable. A few questions your team might ask are:

- What common titles, phrases, and terms do we use that conflict with the ethos of a peer-based culture?
- What vocabulary do we use that nudges us back to the ways of dominator hierarchy?
- What better terms can we use that will consistently realign our structure and system toward a decentralized way of functioning?

## Learn From Others

Most people who have overcome physically debilitating issues were only able to do so by educating themselves about possible therapies and treatments and then following through by putting in the hard work to get back on their feet. The leadership scandals of recent years have given rise to several books that are proving helpful to get us where we need to go. Here are but a few such texts:

- *A Church Called TOV: Forming a Goodness Culture That Resists Abuses of Power and Promotes Healing* by Scot McKnight and Laura Barringer (Tyndale Elevate, 2020)
- *Leading Together: The Holy Possibility of Harmony and Synergy in the Face of Change* by Bryan D. Sims (100 Movements Publishing, 2022)
- *The Starfish and The Spirit: Unleashing the Leadership Potential*

*of Churches and Organizations* by Lance Ford, Rob Wegner, and Alan Hirsch (Zondervan Exponential Series, 2021)

- *When Narcissism Comes to Church: Healing Your Community from Emotional and Spiritual Abuse* by Chuck DeGroat (InterVarsity Press, 2020)
- *Canoeing the Mountains: Christian Leadership in Uncharted Territory* by Tod Bolsinger (InterVarsity Press, 2018)
- *UnLeader: Reimagining Leadership and Why We Must* by Lance Ford (Beacon Hill Press, 2012)
- *Redeeming Power: Understanding Authority and Abuse In the Church* by Diane Langberg (Brazos Press, 2020)

Consider making these "book and discussion club" selections for the church staff so you continually form and recalibrate hearts and minds in alignment with Jesus, as Head of his church.

## MAKING DECISIONS AS A BODY

A huge challenge in making the shifts I'm proposing is for leaders to let go of control and instead make decisions together as a body. But for us to see such a transition take place, we must see a loosening of the grip on leadership at every level.

### Lead by Convictions, Not Control

Organizational cultures based on management systems tend to control most aspects of the work, refusing to allow their team members to make decisions or act independently. This results in a lack of delegation, an expectation of excessive reporting, and a feeling of powerlessness among team members. Micromanagers often hoard skills and knowledge, seeing them as a source of personal power and control. But an organization can dispense with command-and-control management when it has a clear purpose and shared principles spelled out in definitive policies and procedures. Identifying such "convictions" together can significantly help all members understand how to align their actions with the organization's goals.

When policies and procedures are defined jointly, it leads to a decentralized movement where the organization's beliefs become a lively, active part of its culture. The organization lives and breathes a set of agreements based on a mutual commitment to what it believes. We want to create a culture that releases control to the places nearest to where the work is done. To accomplish this, well-thought-out policies and practices are crucial. My encouragement is to develop and adapt a set of commitments and policies.

## Create a Culture Where Permission Is a Given

In leadership cultures that "lord over" others, who is allowed to do what is based on seniority, pecking order, and rank. In God's kingdom-based leadership, freedom abounds. Yet, freedom does not mean a lack of responsibility. To the contrary. The greater the freedom in a culture, the greater the need for personal responsibility and accountability. This is the strength of a decentralized, peer-based leadership culture. No one escapes accountability, regardless of tenure and role. Not only does this hold less experienced team members responsible for their decisions and actions, but the most accomplished and recognized voices in the organization must also answer for their choices and behavior.

Below are some key principles for creating an environment of freedom and permission.

- **Trust people:** You will never see the best work from someone who must constantly seek approval. Policies that slow the competently gifted people in our midst communicate a lack of confidence in our people and stifle creativity, risk-taking, and progress.
- **Let others do it their way:** A sure way to kill the spirit of someone is to invoke the age-old, "This is the way we do it

here." The greatest breakthroughs in industry, technology, and science would never have come about with such thinking. There is no limit to examples of this. If you love rock 'n' roll, you need to give thanks for Les Paul, the inventor of the electric guitar. He dreamed of a better guitar than the centuries-old acoustic version everyone used and was laughed at by those around him as he worked to create a new type of instrument. Long live Les Paul!

- **Let teams and individuals set their own goals:** Organizations with a management culture too often set and pass goals "down" to others—not to be questioned or evaluated, but to be met. Such practices eliminate ownership and deny the insight and creativity of those closest to the task or issue at hand. In cultures of trust, folks will often set higher and better goals for themselves than those coming from hierarchical overseers. Ownership of goals begins with people setting their "own" goals.

Realigning to our true Atlas requires a determined dedication to a collaborative approach to leadership based on the cell-like structure of the human body. The idea is for the body of Christ to create a network of interconnected and interdependent teams, where each team functions as an autonomous unit. The equipper's role becomes that of a facilitator and coach, providing guidance and support while encouraging the team members to generate and contribute their own ideas. This decentralized structure eliminates the traditional hierarchical and command-and-control model, leading to a more inclusive approach to decision-making. By fostering a sense of ownership and responsibility among team members, this cell-like structure can lead to improved and more dynamic leadership. The collective intelligence and creativity of all team members are harnessed to achieve shared goals, resulting in a stronger and more effective organization. Again, the wisdom of the Head is disseminated into the body.

## Develop and Commit to an Advice Process

In organizations that value mutual submission, a common practice is the use of an "advice process." This is a straightforward mechanism that allows anyone in the organization to make decisions, but they must first seek advice from all relevant parties and experts on the matter.

The person making the decision isn't obligated to follow every piece of advice they receive, but they should seriously consider it and think about how the decision will impact others in the organization.

Traditionally, decisions are made either by the boss or through consensus. The advice process goes beyond these two methods by giving a larger voice to those affected by the decision or who have a stake in it. This also enables those closest to the issue to make a faster, more informed decision without being bogged down by bureaucracy or the slow pace of consensus.

Of the many benefits of a strong advice process, some are:

- Drawing in those who are asked for advice, making them informed and invested in the decision.
- Demonstrating humility by seeking advice.
- Providing educational opportunities and tapping into the expertise of those in the field.
- Improving the chances of making the best decision.
- Building team spirit and creativity.

It's important to note that the advice process is not the same as consensus. Consensus can slow down progress and can lead to accountability issues, as no one is ultimately responsible for the decision. The advice process, on the other hand, clearly places ownership of the decision with the person making it, who is motivated and enthusiastic about carrying it out and proving the worthiness of their decision. The key to a successful advice process is to ensure that it is transparent, inclusive, and accessible to all stakeholders. Additionally, it is important to have clear rules and procedures in place to ensure that the advice process is effective and that recommendations are considered in decision-making. Here are some areas to consider when implementing an advice process within your team:

## Ground Rules

- **Openness and transparency:** All relevant information should be openly shared so that team members can make well-informed advice.
- **Inclusivity:** Every team member should have an opportunity to participate in the process. No voice is too small or inconsequential.
- **Respect and civility:** Team members must show respect for one another's opinions, even when they disagree.
- **Accountability:** Whoever is responsible for the final decision should be identified upfront, and they are accountable for both seeking and considering advice.
- **Timelines:** Deadlines for advice should be set and adhered to. This helps to keep the process from dragging on and delaying decisions.

## Procedures

- **Formally initiate the process:** Clearly state—whether through an email, a meeting, or a message on your team communication platform—that a decision needs to be made, and that the process is beginning.
- **Identify stakeholders:** Make a list of people who will be impacted by the decision and therefore should be included in the advice process.
- **Set a deadline:** Specify how long the advice process will remain open for input. Make sure this is a reasonable but defined period.
- **Collect advice:** Utilize tools like surveys, direct consultations, or even group meetings to collect advice from team members.

- **Document feedback:** Collect all the advice and feedback in a single document or platform, so it's easy to review and consider.
- **Review and analyze:** The person or group responsible for the decision reviews all the advice received. They can ask for clarification or additional information if needed.
- **Make the decision:** The responsible person/group should then make a final decision based on the advice received.
- **Communicate the outcome:** Once the decision is made, it should be communicated to all stakeholders, along with a summary of how the advice was considered in the decision-making process.
- **Review and reflect:** After the decision is implemented, it's good practice to evaluate the outcome and the effectiveness of the advice process. This is the time to make adjustments for future iterations of the process.
- **Document the process:** Keep a record of how the advice process unfolded for future reference and to use in orienting new team members.

By adhering to these ground rules and procedures, your team can foster an advice process that is not only effective but also inclusive and transparent.

## Make Decisions Through the Advice Process

The prevailing method for significant decision-making in most churches is for the senior and executive pastor to make decisions in a closed office and then give orders to "junior" leaders. This is the way of playing Atlas, which circumvents the government of the church being on the shoulders of Jesus. But making decisions through the advice process eliminates this "top-down" approach. Even leaders used to operating in rank-based systems as "senior" or the Big Boss, need to be bound by the advice process. This gives everyone on the team a voice in significant decisions. The hope, especially for wide-ranging decisions, is for the team to be able to say, "It seemed good to the apostles and elders, with the whole church, to ..." (Acts 15:22). This quote from Acts comes from the Council at Jerusalem, where the fledgling church was dealing with the weighty issue of whether circumcision was needed for salvation. Notable apostolic leaders and elders, along with a multitude from the church, gathered to discuss the matter.

It should be pointed out that this account is often used as a proof text by those who advocate for a singular decision-maker. After much debate and at a quiet time in the discussion, James spoke up. After sharing his viewpoint, he said, "Therefore it is my judgment ..." (Acts 15:19). According to some, this proves that James was the final decision-maker. However, a careful look at the text shows that James was simply sharing his opinion on the matter. The process the leadership undertook to come to their final decision is shown in verse 28: "It seemed good to the Holy Spirit and to us." James did not write the Council's letter to the Gentile believers, and the letter does not say that James had made the final judgment on the matter. They believed that the voice of the Holy Spirit came through the collective voice of the apostles, elders, and gathered church.

Lesser decisions do not require the same volume of advice-seeking required for wide-reaching decisions, but they do require an advice process. Encourage your team members to ask for input from the right people before making a decision that affects others on their team or in the organization. They don't have to follow every piece of advice, but they should listen to what others have to say. The bigger the decision, the more input they should get. The person who sees the issue or opportunity, or who it affects the most, gets to make the call. There is no need for managers to get involved or for decisions to be slowed down by committees. The advice process finds a happy middle ground—those affected get a say, but decisions can still happen quickly.

Below are some key principles for executing the advice process:

- Encourage team members to always seek advice from relevant parties and experts before making any decision.

- Identify a specific opportunity or challenge.
- Ensure the scope of the advice sought is directly proportional to the magnitude of the decision.
- Be clear that the decision-making authority lies with the person who identified the opportunity or challenge, or who is most impacted by it.
- Seek input from relevant parties and experts.
- Consider the advice received.
- Understand that the person making the decision is not obligated to integrate every piece of advice, but it should be taken into consideration.
- See the preceding steps as a balance between hierarchical authority and consensus-based approaches—ensuring efficient decision-making while giving all stakeholders a voice.
- Make the decision, taking into account the input received.

One bonus a dedicated advice process brings is *greater* accountability. For instance, when Debra—who is the point person for local missions in her church—is considering an outreach for the Christmas season, she works through the advice process and is willing to give an account for her final decisions on how the budget was spent and who was served through the outreach. Collaboration through a decentralized structure doesn't decrease accountability and responsibility; instead, it spreads them evenly among all members of the organization. Instead of being accountable only to a single supervisor or manager, individuals are now responsible to their peers. This shift in the traditional hierarchy creates an organic hierarchy. It is an inclusive approach, where all members of the team have a greater sense of ownership and responsibility for their actions and decisions.

## Forbid the Use of Force or Threats

Exercising dominion over others (Jesus' words) is the use of *power* over one another. If you have not experienced it yourself, you have most likely heard of or witnessed firsthand a church staff member being verbally dressed down or unilaterally fired by a "senior" leader. I have heard of many people getting fired suddenly without mediation or recourse. I have seen people who were the main or significant financial provider for their families dismissed from their station of calling by irrational, insecure, or vindictive leaders who had the power to shatter the world of another fellow disciple, another servant of Jesus.

We need to seriously think about this. Jesus definitively commanded that we are not to exercise domination over one another in his kingdom. However, it has become widely acceptable for one or two people to shun a person who has answered the call of God to serve a local body. This affects not only the individual being fired but also their entire family, who have also become embedded in the faith community. And of course, the wider church family is also affected. Where did we get the idea that one person has the God-ordained authority to summarily dismiss a fellow servant from their place of calling? We certainly did not get it from the New Testament.

We have become so accustomed to the worldly notions of bosses and subordinates that we fail to recognize the degree to which such ideas conflict with Jesus. Such ideology is a petri dish for abuse—the very abuse that has dominated the media concerning churches and faith-based organizations in recent years. Sadly, the most common solution proposed is to try for more and *better* leadership and account-ability, rather than questioning and deeply analyzing the system itself. We have sowed to the wind and reaped the whirlwind in this regard. Scandal upon scandal has been the harvest reaped from such "leadership" seeds.

## Develop a Conflict-Resolution Policy and Process

Jesus lays out a detailed process in Matthew 18:15–20 that provides fundamental steps for navigating disputable matters or issues that arise among his followers.

Many large corporations (those over one hundred employees) operate via decentralized leadership using the method of handling conflict similar to the teaching of Christ. For instance, at Morning Star, a major producer of diced tomatoes and tomato paste in the US, an accountability process is activated in situations of conflict between employees. Despite having a workforce of 400–2,400 people (depending on the season) and operating with two hundred trucks and three processing plants, Morning Star does not have a management team or an HR department. Yet, they still manage to effectively handle conflicts that arise within the company.

Employees at Morning Star make the following commitments to one another:

1.  Have a direct conversation with the person. No gossiping. No backbiting allowed. Anyone noticing a coworker with performance or integrity issues in conflict with the company's values is required to discuss the issue directly with their coworker. If a person is unwilling to initiate a discussion along these lines, then they just have to live with it.

2.  If the one-on-one conversation does not bring resolution, then another person is brought into the discussion as a mediator. This person must be trusted by both colleagues, listen to both parties, clarify what they have heard, and share their thoughts on points made by both coworkers. The mediator is not an arbiter who decides. The power and resolution continue to be in the hands of the two coworkers. The mediator keeps the conversation on track and facilitates mutual understanding. Some differences of opinion don't end in a resolution, especially if one colleague asks another to terminate their own employment.

3.  If differences of opinion among coworkers can't be resolved, a panel of three colleagues is convened to listen to both sides and pursue the conversation until resolution.

Author Doug Kirkpatrick writes, "If the panel become deadlocked, the company owner participates in the deliberations and renders a final decision. At some point, all disputes must come to an end."[4]

The Morning Star process leaves out the last step a faith-based organization might take—bringing the issue to the entire group (whole church). In the church's sphere, since Jesus is the "owner," we must find a solution if we reach step three apart from a resolution. In such scenarios, the person leading the team in the particular department or sphere normally makes the final decision. However, if the conflict-resolution process has been practiced and honored, this last step will rarely be necessary.

The underlying principle we are committing to here is the spirit of *mutual submission*—over and against hierarchical submission. Our overarching objective is to be led by the true Head of the church. In *The Starfish and The Spirit*, Alan Hirsch writes:

> In seeking to remain true to the calling and purpose of the church, we together must seek to look, act, and sound like Jesus. To do this, we have to learn to think like Jesus. In the words of Scripture, this means to seek the mind of Christ in and through the Spirit of Christ (1 Cor. 2:6–16). It is through the Spirit of God that we, together and as individuals, can access the inner rationality of Christ. This is not just access to a theo-logic as if it involved some abstract rational process, but rather is thinking through the lens of Christo-logic, the thought processes of the very Person who rules the universe. This is part of the treasure that the church has access to in Christ (Col. 2:1–5).[5]

## Develop a Dismissal Process

Whether an individual should remain as a staff or team member is one "conflict" issue that will inevitably arise. If nobody has the unilateral

---

[4]  Doug Kirkpatrick, *Beyond Empowerment: The Age of the Self-Managed Organization* (Scotts Valley, CA: CreateSpace, 2011), 31.

[5]  Ford, et al., *The Starfish and the Spirit*, 281.

authority to fire another individual, then how might we deal with such situations? Consider adopting a dismissal process that everyone agrees to when they come aboard the staff or team.

From the onset of employment, we can require that everyone agree to the standards of the team's culture and the practice of mutual submission. The team should draft a statement outlining these agreements, including a reference to conditions that might lead to dismissal. (See sample language under "Step 1" below.)

Then, if any team member feels a fellow worker should leave the team, they must first initiate the conflict-resolution process with the possibility of dismissal on the table. This means the person who is offended, claims to have verifiable information, or has strong feelings as to why another servant should be dismissed, honors their own commitment to mutual submission by bringing those concerns to fellow team members. This process promotes a sense of fairness and equity in the workplace by eliminating impulsive termination decisions made by a single individual or a small group of individuals in positions of authority. Furthermore, for a servant struggling with their performance, it provides a valuable opportunity—rather than being fired, they can be offered the chance to explore alternative roles within the church or organization that align more closely with their unique gifts, talents, and abilities. Ultimately, though, there are times when an individual is just not a suitable fit for their position, and this method of termination through an accountability and conflict-resolution process can help them reach that realization in a constructive and supportive manner.

After going through this process, the individual in question will either leave the team or will be offered another role that better fits their giftings, talents, skills, and calling. In cases of outright sinful behavior that reaches an untenable state or in situations where the group is convinced that the person's contribution to the mission should end, those remaining at the conflict-resolution table are tasked with making that final decision.

Another possible outcome is that the person stays in their role because the conflict-resolution process reveals the issue is not with this individual, but instead is with the person who raised it.

Below is a step-by-step outline of a healthy conflict-resolution process that includes the possibility of a dismissal.

**Step 1: Agreement to a culture and practice of mutual submission.** All team members must agree to the culture and practice of mutual submission from the onset of employment. This means that they acknowledge that decisions about staff or team members are made with the collective voice of the team and that they agree to be mutually submitted to the counsel and voice of the Lord as manifested in their fellow servants in all matters that affect them mutually, including a person's ongoing place on the staff or team. This step lays the foundation for a fair and equitable dismissal process that everyone has agreed to.

**Step 2: Conflict-resolution process initiation.** If any team member feels that a fellow worker should leave the team, they must first initiate the conflict-resolution process. This process should be followed to ensure that all perspectives are considered and that any termination decisions are made constructively and collaboratively. By doing so, impulsive termination decisions made by a single individual or a small group of individuals in positions of authority can be avoided, promoting a sense of fairness and equity in the workplace.

**Step 3: Self-reflection.** The individual in question will be given an opportunity to reflect on their performance and explore alternative roles within the organization that align more closely with their unique gifts, talents, and abilities. This step is important because it provides an opportunity for growth and development, and it allows the individual to better understand their strengths and weaknesses and how they can contribute to the organization in a meaningful way. As alluded to in the previous section, the conflict-resolution process may have revealed the problem is not the fault of the person at the focus of the process, but of the person who initiated the process.

*Step 4: Final decision by the conflict resolution table.* If the situation reaches an untenable state or if the group is convinced that the individual's contribution to the mission should end, the remaining members at the conflict-resolution table will be tasked with offering a final decision. This step is necessary to ensure that the team's mission and values are upheld and that the team can continue to operate effectively and efficiently.

*Step 5: Alternative role or termination.* Based on the final decision, the individual in question will either leave the team or be offered another role that better fits their giftings, talents, skills, and calling. If, however, the process reveals there is no issue with the person at the center of the process, they will continue in their role. This step ensures that the individual's unique strengths and abilities are utilized to their fullest potential, while also ensuring that the team's goals and objectives are met.

*Step 6: Closure.* The dismissal process ends, and all parties involved move forward in a constructive and supportive manner. This step is important to ensure that everyone can move past any negative experiences and that the team can continue to operate in a positive and productive environment that honors the Lord.

Endeavoring to get things right as leaders in the church cannot be overemphasized. Jesus is the Head of his church. Our responsibility to reflect his glory calls us to stop trying to take his place and to remove all barriers to the free flow of his life and expression throughout his body. As you move forward in your leadership journey, my encouragement is that not only is it possible to change the current system, but that we *must* change it. We must at least try—as much as it depends on us. And what most depends on us is to constantly check our alignment with our true Atlas—Jesus, the Head of the church. The hope, joy, and fruitfulness of being stewards of the Lord's gifts and callings to his followers is at stake here. It is far past time that we stop trying to tweak or adjust a system that was never intended for the church in the first place. It is time to cease allowing the abuse and destruction of countless individuals, families, and entire churches under a false leadership rubric that provides platforms and safe havens for "leaders" who have hijacked Jesus as Atlas of his own body.

Celebrity-ism has no place in the church. Jesus alone is due the credit and applause. May we give all the time we have to do all within us to shine the light on him and from him. To God be all glory and honor and power, forever. It must be so on our watch.

# ACKNOWLEDGMENTS

At the end of the day, a book like this is the accumulation of thoughts, ideas, opinions, experiences, and conclusions (at least by the time of publication!) of the author. And many helpful and thoughtful people deserve thanks for making it possible for me to bring those categories to ink on paper.

It has been said the best critique of the bad is the practice of the better. When you have experienced the good, it is a lot easier to recognize the bad. I am forever thankful for my years with the faithful people in Rolla, Missouri at Family Fellowship Church. It was there that I experienced the greatest expression of humble servanthood from women and men who were genuine elders among us all.

Thank you, Susan and Gary Broyles, George Wilson, Pat and Dick Rechtien, Jane and Dave Easter, Kay and Dave Thomas, and Gus Mauller. Gary, George, Dick, Jane, and Gus have passed on, and I lament not being able to hear their voices in my ear, yet I continue to do so in my heart.

Thank you, Alan Hirsch, for so many years of mentorship and friendship; Neil Cole, for being a voice crying in the wilderness; and Rob Wegner, for deep friendship and the diamond of integrity you are.

Thank you, Brenna Varner, Joel Varner, and Anna Robinson, for your hard work in the entire process of making this book a reality. None of you let me get lazy when you were able.

And finally, a huge thank you to Dr. Eddie Weller, who sparked an idea that became this work.

# RESOURCES FOR REALIGNING

If you'd like to delve deeper into *The Atlas Factor* and learn how to effectively apply its principles, processes, and practices within your church or organization, we invite you to explore our website at www. theatlasfactor.com.

## CONSULTATION AND TRAINING OPPORTUNITIES

If you're interested in hosting a seminar, retreat, or consultation, or if you're seeking long-term training for your team or organization, please don't hesitate to get in touch with us. We're here to support your journey toward realignment.

## FREE RESOURCES

Visit our website to access a wealth of complementary resources, including insightful videos, concise white papers, and downloadable PDFs containing all the Team Process questions from *The Atlas Factor*. These resources are designed to empower you and your group on your realignment journey.

## SPEAKING ENGAGEMENTS WITH LANCE FORD

If you've found *The Atlas Factor* valuable and would like Lance to share his expertise at your church, conference, or event, we welcome your inquiries. Feel free to reach out to Lance directly via email at lance@ theatlasfactor.com.

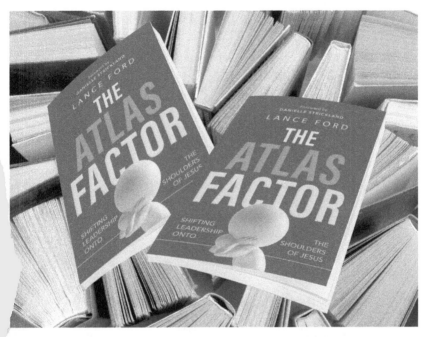